PERSONAL BANKRUPTCY:

A GUIDE TO CONTROLLING RUNAWAY DEBT

By Jeffrey Freedman, Esq.

Revised 1997

Acknowledgements

It is difficult to express how much I have learned from having represented over 10,000 families with debt problems since 1977. Their view of the bankruptcy process has shaped many parts of this book.

A number of the members of my staff offered comments at various stages of this book and made themselves available to share insights into the bankruptcy system; among them Ken Hiller, Paul Pochepan, Barbara Kraemer and Darlene Craig. I also offer thanks to Mark Segal of Segal & McMahan, Las Vegas, and William F. Savino of Damon & Morey LLP, Buffalo, for their guidance. And most important of all, I want to acknowledge the support of my wife, Barbara, who accepted my unusual work schedule.

This book, now in its third edition, is intended as a basic guide to consumer bankruptcy law. It provides answers to routine questions and issues that most frequently arise when dealing with the subject.

This is a dynamic and changing area of the law, with new developments nearly every month. Many issues regarding consumer bankruptcy have not been fully settled, and will continue to be the subject of litigation and appellate court opinions.

This book is not intended to be a definitive treatment of consumer bankruptcy law. However, it can serve as a guide to issues and trends in the law as it exists. Reliance on any statements made herein should not be a substitute for an attorney's independent research and judgment.

About the Author

Jeffrey M. Freedman is the senior partner and founding attorney of Jeffrey Freedman Attorneys at Law. The law firm's practice is concentrated in the areas of bankruptcy, Social Security Disability and personal injury law.

Mr. Freedman graduated from American University in Washington, D.C., and earned his law degree at Western New England College School of Law in Springfield, Massachusetts.

He served as a Chapter 7 Trustee with the Bankruptcy Court for seven years and has practiced law in the Western New York area since 1977. Since opening the firm in 1980, he has assisted more than 10,000 families with debt problems and has helped more than 3,000 clients obtain Social Security Disability benefits. In addition, his firm has obtained millions of dollars for clients who have been injured in accidents.

He is a member of the Monroe County and Erie County bar associations, the New York State Bar Association, American Bar Association, the Monroe County Bar Association Bankruptcy Committee, Erie County Bar Association Commercial Law Committee, the New York State Bar Association Special Committee on Lawyer Advertising and Referral Services, the National Organization of Social Security Claimants' Representatives, and the New York State Trial Lawyers' Association. He is former vice president and a founding member of the National Association of Consumer Bankruptcy Attorneys, and an associate member of the National Association of Chapter 13 Trustees.

In addition, he has been the recipient of both the New York State Bar Association Pro Bono Award and the Erie County Bar Association Pro Bono Award.

Mr. Freedman has been quoted on legal topics by several upstate publications, including the *Democrat and Chronicle, Rochester Business Journal, The Buffalo News, Business First,* the *New York State Bar Association Journal,* and the American Bankruptcy Institute's *Journal.* He has also lectured before many national, state and local groups, and has appeared on numerous radio and television talk shows.

A special thank you to my wife, Barbara, whose patience and support helped make this project a success.

Table of Contents

Introduction

Joe Smith* could barely get a brief "hello" out of his mouth as he and his wife came into my office. He sat on the edge of the chair across the desk from me, while his wife, with white knuckles clutching her handbag in her lap, began to talk about their financial situation.

Mrs. Smith spoke about how the debts had piled up after her husband's employer went out of business and Joe lost his job. As Mrs. Smith told the story of their debt problems, Joe began to perspire. I noticed a slight tremor in his hands as he reached for the pamphlet on Chapter 7 Bankruptcy and Chapter 13, which I offered to help explain the couple's options.

> When I see clients in my office for the first time, they are usually scared to death.

When I see clients in my office for the first time, they are usually scared to death. The thought of filing bankruptcy or Chapter 13 is frightening, yet the majority of clients who file do so because of circumstances beyond their control. Many are going through a divorce, have been laid off from their job or have had medical problems or a business failure that has put them in a rough financial situation.

When I first meet with prospective clients, I reassure them that this is not the end of the world. Facing bankruptcy is traumatic, but it is possible to put your life back together, and regain both your financial stability and your happiness.

Once the client feels more comfortable, we move on to the next step in the process — analyzing the debt problems. The answers to a few simple questions help me learn how to direct the client:

- Can the employment situation be improved?
- What are the monthly expenses, and can they be decreased?
- What are the amount and type of debt?
- What kind of assets does the family own and what are they worth?

Many times, after doing this analysis, I find that a bankruptcy would not be appropriate. I refer that person to a local agency such as the Consumer Credit Counseling Service or the Cornell Cooperative Extension for help.

* Although the situations described are real, the names of the persons in this book have been changed to protect confidentiality.

Many of the clients we see end up filing Chapter 7 or Chapter 13 because they are simply unable to make the payments their creditors require, or are unable to work out a payment plan with creditors.

Most clients think that if they file Chapter 7 or Chapter 13 they will lose everything. That's just not true. Filing bankruptcy in most cases allows the debtor to keep his or her home, car and personal property.

If my clients could describe bankruptcy in one word after they have completed the process, that word would be "hope." Hope has been restored to the future of a person who once felt totally overwhelmed by his or her financial situation.

One way of looking at the compassion of a country is to look at its bankruptcy statutes. Life has not been good to the people who walk into my office. It gives me a satisfying feeling to be able to use those bankruptcy statutes to do something that relieves the serious problems these people are facing.

The present bankruptcy system gives debtors a chance to start over. The number of bankruptcy filings has grown significantly in the past decade. Bankruptcy is as American as apple pie, and is likely to be a permanent and growing feature as we move towards the 21st century.

This book will answer many of the questions that arise in filing Chapter 7 (Bankruptcy) and Chapter 13 (the Wage Earner's Plan). If you, like the Smiths, are under tremendous pressure due to your current financial situation, I hope you will not only find this book helpful, but that you will be relieved of some of your fears.

Jeffrey M. Freedman

Jeffrey M. Freedman

1

The Fresh Start Option

Bob Warren was 61 years old. His wife, Mary, age 60, got up at 5 each morning to go to work at McDonald's. When they came into my office, facing bankruptcy, I asked them, "Whatever happened to the golden years?"

"The golden years," Bob said, "have turned to lead."

Bob, you see, was disabled with a medical condition that prevented him from working and required the use of some very expensive medications. Because their medical insurance did not include coverage for prescriptions, Bob and Mary had to use credit cards to pay for the medications. They wanted to pay their creditors, but had no means of increasing their income to cover the cost of the medicine. Eventually Bob and Mary ended up with credit card bills that they could not repay — their golden years had truly become a burden.

Nearly everyone, at some time in life, faces financial problems. If this happens to you, it's important to consider all your options. Debt counseling is often the first step, but when the situation is desperate, you may need to file a Chapter 7 bankruptcy petition or a Chapter 13 Wage Earner's Plan.

We can trace the concept of bankruptcy back to the Bible in which a forgiveness of debt is recommended every seven years. Today, it is a legal proceeding that enables you to:

- wipe out all or most of your debt (although debts such as child support, fines, some taxes and some student loans can be exceptions)

- keep your house and allow you to catch up on missed payments

- prevent your car from being repossessed

- stop wage garnishment and creditor harassment resulting from collection efforts

As part of our legal system, the U.S. Constitution grants the federal government the power to make bankruptcy laws (Article 1, Sec. 8 (1787)). Until recently, bankruptcy has carried a social stigma, often considered to be a skeleton that was best kept in the closet.

During the 1980s and 1990s, however, such big names as Kim Basinger, Mickey Rooney, Tammy Wynette, Wayne Newton, Continental Airlines and many other well-known, well-respected businesses and individuals sought protection in bankruptcy court. Bankruptcy has come out of the closet. Its power to discharge debt and give the individual or business a chance for financial rebirth is recognized as a valuable part of our legal system.

But people are still ambivalent about bankruptcy. The circumstances leading to financial problems seem to have a great deal to do with how bankruptcy is accepted by our society. For someone who is laid off from a job and has a family to support, who has many medical expenses, or who goes through a divorce, the option of bankruptcy is socially more acceptable than for the person who has purchased expensive stereo equipment and used credit cards to eat out every day of the week.

Debt problems bring on feelings of anger, disbelief, helplessness, despair, guilt, shame, anxiety, confusion and frustration — no matter what their origin. These feelings are often made worse by a sense of isolation — that you are the only one with these kinds of problems.

Debt problems bring on feelings of anger, disbelief, helplessness, despair, guilt, shame, anxiety, confusion and frustration

As we discussed earlier, you are not alone. More and more people are becoming overburdened with debt. In the last few years, between 800,000 and one million cases have been filed annually. At that rate, nearly 4,000 cases are filed *every business day* in the U.S. Debt pushes many people over the brink when an unexpected event such as a family breakup, illness, layoff or business failure occurs. Other individuals simply have lost ground because of inflation.

Chapter 7 bankruptcy and Chapter 13, the Wage Earner's Plan, are last-resort options. Straight bankruptcy or Chapter 7 allows an honest debtor to have the court "discharge" or cancel most of his or her debts in order to obtain a fresh start. The Wage Earner's Plan is an alternative to straight bankruptcy, and lets you pay off part or all of your debts under court supervision over three to five years.

If you have a steady income, either as a wage earner, owner of a small business, or as a recipient of a pension or benefits from Social Security or welfare, you may be able to file Chapter 13.

Those who file Chapter 7 will have the bankruptcy on their credit record for nine years and nine months. Chapter 13 stays on your credit record for six years and nine months. However, most people who file already have a poor credit record, and many have a judgment or other negative information on their record that will remain for the same six years and nine months.

We do not encourage people to go into bankruptcy or to file a Chapter 13 plan. We look at all their options and refer them to credit counseling services if we think that will help. There are many cases, however, where bankruptcy is the only way out of overburdening debt. Bankruptcy exists to give relief to those who need it most. It is a valuable legal right for making a fresh start and freeing debtors from creditor harassment as well as the worries and pressures of too much debt.

After you've filed for bankruptcy to get a fresh start, life goes on. You will have the freedom to move, open a bank account, keep all the wages you earn, buy a house or car, apply for credit, or start a business.

Re-establishing credit will take you several years. But, if you haven't been paying your bills on time, your credit rating is probably already poor. Filing bankruptcy will not make it much worse.

> We do not encourage people to go into bankruptcy or to file a Chapter 13 plan

2

Filing Chapter 7 Bankruptcy

When I first began practicing law, one of my clients brought out a Visa card when it came time to pay the court filing fee. I had to tell him neither the court nor Jeffrey Freedman Attorneys at Law takes Visa, MasterCard or Diners Club. This is one occasion you can also leave your American Express card at home.

It's almost a contradiction in terms, but it does cost money to file bankruptcy. First there is a court filing fee, which at this writing is $175 but is subject to change. In addition, attorney fees range from $500 to $1,000 or more (1997). If you have been involved in a business, own a home and need judgment liens avoided, or have a case that will be time-consuming due to other complications, the attorney fees will be higher.

Some people consider filing bankruptcy themselves, without using an attorney. Our law firm doesn't recommend this, and that's not just because bankruptcy cases are a big part of our law practice.

> **There are many pitfalls to filing bankruptcy on your own**

There are many pitfalls to filing bankruptcy on your own. If you should forget, for instance, to list one of your creditors on your petition, you could end up having to pay that creditor back. The fee you pay an attorney can be well worth it when you consider the cost of making a mistake on your petition.

Also, getting through the filing on your own could be a time-consuming, confusing process. Attorneys who deal with the bankruptcy courts on a regular basis know how to do things correctly, and how to get them done in a timely manner.

Once your petition has been filed, you will be required to attend a hearing, which usually takes place several weeks after the filing. The court or trustee will notify you by mail, about three weeks before the hearing, of the date, time and place to attend.

At your hearing the court-appointed trustee will question you about your finances for about five minutes. If you've filed a joint petition with your spouse, he or she must also attend the hearing.

As we have stated before, you can file bankruptcy if you have been sued, have a judgment against you, have bills in collection agencies, have had a repossession, have had your wages attached or have any other debt problems. Once you have filed, all harassment from creditors will stop.

Here's what happens in a simple Chapter 7 bankruptcy:

Step 1: You meet once or twice with your attorney, who takes information to process the Chapter 7 petition.

Step 2: The legal fee and disbursements are paid in full, then the attorney completes the petition.

Step 3: A legal secretary types the petition.

Step 4: You return to the office to review and sign the petition.

Step 5: Your petition is filed with the Bankruptcy Court and a filing fee of $175 is paid to the court. Your petition will include a detailed list of your debts, all your assets and any exemptions you claim.

The Bankruptcy Court then assigns your file a case number, and the automatic stay (which prevents creditors from harassing you) takes effect.

Step 6: A copy of your petition is mailed to you, which you should examine and keep for your records.

Step 7: The court schedules a 341 Meeting (the meeting of your creditors), to take place within 20 to 40 days after you have filed. You and your creditors are notified of the meeting, which you are required to attend. This may be the only time you must appear at a hearing.

The court notification contains several important facts: the date of your filing, the date of the 341 Meeting, the case number, the trustee, the judge, where the meeting will be held, the last day on which a creditor can file an objection to the discharge, and the last day on which a creditor can file a complaint to determine dischargeability of a debt. For residents of Monroe, Ontario, Livingston, Wayne, Seneca and Yates counties, the meeting will be at the U.S. Courthouse, 100 State St., Rochester; if you live in Steuben, Schuyler, Orleans, Genesee, Wyoming or Chemung counties, the meeting is at the Schuyler County Courthouse, N. Franklin St., Watkins Glen. This notice is mailed to you and all the creditors listed on your bankruptcy schedules. The law assumes the creditors will receive the notice if their names and addresses are correctly listed on your bankruptcy schedule.

Step 8: The meeting of creditors is run by the trustee appointed to your case. He or she asks you some questions about how the papers were filed, asks about your property, and verifies the statements in the petition. Usually, most creditors do not attend the meeting.

Step 9: Your creditors have 60 days from your 341 Meeting to file an objection to your discharge or to claim that certain debts are non-dischargeable.

Step 10: Unless your creditors have objected (in most of the cases there are no objections), about 60 days after your 341 Meeting you receive a discharge. Your notice of discharge is a document that prevents your creditors from collecting the debts listed in your bankruptcy papers. Your case is officially closed, and the trustee files his report with the court.

What is the purpose of the 341 Meeting when a Chapter 7 is filed?

The primary function of the 341 Meeting is to provide the trustee an opportunity to question the debtor under oath regarding various aspects of the bankruptcy case.

How long will I be at the 341 Meeting?

Your actual involvement will only be 5 to 10 minutes. However, there are usually many cases scheduled, and therefore, you may have to wait anywhere from 30 to 90 minutes before your case is called by the trustee.

What questions are asked at the 341 Meeting?

Each trustee has his or her own style and could ask a variety of other questions as well. Exactly what will be asked will depend on the facts of the particular case. In addition, the order of questions will be determined by the trustee.

Typical questions include:

Your attorney is showing you your bankruptcy petition.
- Did you sign all places required?
- Did you list all of your assets?
- Did you list all of your debts?

The trustee will then review the assets you listed in the petition, and may have questions about the assets and their value.

The trustee will review the 15 answers given in the Statement of Financial Affairs and may have a few questions about the Statement of Affairs.

**If real estate is owned, the following
questions might be asked:**

- How did you arrive at the value of your home?
- When did you buy the home?
- What are the mortgage and/or home equity loan balances?
- Have you made any significant improvements to the home since you purchased it?

**If a motor vehicle is owned, the following
questions may be asked:**

- May I see a copy of your title?
- How did you arrive at the value of the motor vehicle?
- What is the balance due on the motor vehicle?

**The following four questions are now required following the
passage of the Bankruptcy Reform Act of 1994 which took effect
on October 22, 1994:**

- Are you aware of the potential consequences of filing bankruptcy?
- Are you aware of the fact that you could have filed under other Chapters of the Bankruptcy Code?
- Are you aware of the effect of the bankruptcy discharge?
- Are you aware of the effect of reaffirming a debt?

The purpose of the last four questions is solely informational and is not intended to be an interrogation to which the client must provide specific answers. As a matter of fact, there is no provision in the law to do anything if satisfactory answers are not given to the last four questions.

Rather than asking the above four questions, the Chapter 7 trustee may give you a copy of a memo entitled "Statement of Information Required by 11 U.S.C. §341." He will ask you to read it, and ask if you have any questions.

3

Debts That Remain After Filing Chapter 7

Although Chapter 7 will discharge most of your debts, there are some exceptions.

Read the following carefully, and if you have any similar situations, discuss the problem with your lawyer as soon as possible. It's to your advantage to get all the facts out, and to get them out as soon as possible.

- Credit card debts and open store account charges for luxury goods or services owing to a single creditor and amounting to more than $1000, which have been run up within 60 days prior to filing.

- Cash advances where more than $1,000 has been obtained within 60 days before the case is filed.

- A claim resulting from a car or motorcycle accident where you have injured another party, related to driving while intoxicated (DWI or drunken driving).

- Child support or alimony payments.

- Certain legal fees for the lawyer who represented your spouse or ex-spouse in divorce or support proceedings.

- If you have been divorced, any debts that the judge in the divorce court ordered you to pay. Show your attorney the papers and he or she will try to get you out from under those bills. However, some will have to be paid or you may be held in contempt by the divorce court judge.

- The reasonable value of an item you may have sold before you finished paying for it and pledged as collateral. For instance, if you had a stereo you owed $500 on, sold the stereo for $400 (which was what it was worth on the market), and used the money to pay other bills or buy food, you might still owe the creditor the $400.

- Checks you have written that have "bounced" and are still being held by the creditor. These must still be listed in the bankruptcy petition. It is best to pay these, because you could be charged with a crime if you don't.

- Debts incurred to pay certain taxes with borrowed funds may be nondischargeable as well.

- Student loans you have received through a college you attended, or a bank, that were guaranteed by the U.S. government or by a state. Student loans can be discharged if it has been more than seven years from the date your first payment was due. If it has been less than seven years since you began payments, the loan can be discharged only if you can prove that the debt places an "undue hardship" on yourself or your dependents. (See Chapter 15 of this book for additional information.)

- Money that has been lent to you by a finance company which has been defrauded.

  Although it sounds far-fetched, you can be accused of defrauding a company that has lent you money if it believes you weren't careful to notify it of your exact financial situation when you took out the loan. When you borrow money, you are asked to give the finance company involved a list of all your creditors. You should always keep a copy of this list.

  If you don't have a copy and file a bankruptcy petition later, the company can claim you did not tell it the true story of your financial situation, and can say you defrauded it. If it sues you, you must defend the case. If it proves you cheated and defrauded the company, you will have to pay back what you borrowed from it.

- Taxes due within the past three years, or for which you filed a false return or no return. Other taxes that you had a fiduciary obligation to collect, such as employee withholding taxes and sales taxes. (See Chapter 16 of this book for additional information.)

You can be accused of defrauding a company that has lent you money if it believes you weren't careful to notify it of your exact financial situation

- Any interest in real estate, a house, a car or personal property which you want to keep, and which you have offered as security on a loan.

- Debts resulting from your taking someone's property without permission, or from fraud or embezzlement.

- Fines and penalties payable to the government, including traffic or parking tickets.

- Also, you may have to pay back debts you have not listed on your bankruptcy petition.

Discharging Your Debts

It is important that you know if all your debts will be discharged. Discuss this with your attorney before your case is filed. In some instances your attorney will know right away. In other cases for a debt to be nondischargeable the creditor would need to sue and your attorney might not know this will happen in advance of the filing.

4

Questions And Concerns About Chapter 7

Naturally, when people first visit my office, they have a lot of questions about bankruptcy. Every once in a while, though, I find I don't have all the answers. For instance, I once had a single lady come in and tell me she wanted to get a fresh start, and she wanted to have a baby. I had to tell her I could help her with the fresh start, but she'd have to talk to someone else about the baby. We are a full-service law firm — but not quite that full-service.

Here are some of the more standard questions I am asked:

Exactly what is bankruptcy?

Bankruptcy is a legal proceeding provided by federal law that allows those who are unable to pay their bills to obtain a fresh start.

What does bankruptcy accomplish?

- It stops wage garnishment and collection harassment.
- Cancels out most debts.
- Stops repossession of property.
- Stops mortgage foreclosure.

Is a court appearance required?

You have to go to a meeting called the "meeting of creditors" to meet with the bankruptcy trustee and any of your creditors who choose to come. Most of the time, the meeting is simple and short. You will be asked a few questions about your case. In most cases creditors do not attend the meeting.

Is it mostly people who "live high" who are involved in personal bankruptcies?

Not at all. Occasionally a celebrity such as a movie star gets publicity for filing bankruptcy, but this is not typical. Usually it is an ordinary working person who has lost his or her job, gone through a divorce, is temporarily disabled or has unexpected high medical bills. These circumstances make it difficult for the person to pay all of his or her creditors.

Are there more personal bankruptcies than business bankruptcies?

Yes. About 90 percent of bankruptcies filed are personal.

Are bankruptcies usually filed for large amounts of money?

No. Usually one creditor is putting the pressure on and demanding all payments at once, including those that are in arrears. The trouble is that all of the debtor's other creditors also want payment, and there just isn't enough money to go around.

Does easy credit contribute to a large number of personal bankruptcies?

Yes. Creditors make it so easy to get credit that we find a number of people become overextended. Often they don't realize how deeply in debt they are, because they keep paying their bills with new loans. Once a person's credit runs out, it's too late. Creditors begin to call and harass them for delinquent payments.

Nearly every day someone walks into my office with a horror story about how credit has been extended to them time and time again, even though they were already way over their heads in debt. Tim Donner owed $50,000 in credit card debt and had 22 credit cards in his name. Mary Burns owed $30,000, and had just received a new, preapproved line of credit in the mail. When she came to my office she had also just received a new, pre-approved card addressed to her father. He had died in 1971.

I have a glass jar in my office that stands about 15 inches tall. On a client's first visit we take all his credit cards, cut them in half and drop them into the jar. Each person usually has between five and 12 cards. The jar is always full.

When is my bankruptcy filing effective?

The moment the court receives the completed petition. When your petition is filed, all suits, wage attachments and other collection activities against you must be stopped. Once you have filed bankruptcy, your attorney will discuss which bills you must pay and the ones you are legally entitled to stop paying.

If I file bankruptcy, will my credit rating be ruined for seven years?

Creditors will often say this to discourage you from filing bankruptcy. There is no federal or state law that prevents you from buying on credit after bankruptcy. Keep in mind that if you are 60 to 90 days behind on your bills, have been sued or had your wages attached, had a repossession, a home foreclosed on or have debts in a collection agency, you probably cannot buy on credit now. According to the Fair Credit Reporting Act, Chapter 7 and Chapter 13 will go on your credit record, and may remain there for 10 years. However, the large local credit reporting firms remove Chapter 7 after nine years and nine months, and Chapter 13 after six years and nine months.

Will filing bankruptcy cause me to lose my job?

That would be most unusual. In most cases your employer won't even know about it. Usually, when an employer knows an employee is having financial problems, it doesn't matter if the employee files bankruptcy, as long as he gets his mind back on the job.

Who will notify my creditors that I have filed bankruptcy?

The court or the trustee will notify your creditors.

What makes people decide to file bankruptcy?

When people feel they are being harassed by creditors at home and at work, they may decide to file bankruptcy to restore peace of mind.

Can my creditors harass me after I have filed bankruptcy?

After your bankruptcy filing your creditors are prohibited from harassing you in any way. They cannot phone you at home or at work, or visit you. However, it can take several weeks before each of your creditors has been told that you have filed bankruptcy and has completely ceased sending you bills or delinquency notices.

Must I list all my bills on my bankruptcy petition?

Yes, you must list them all. However, you can pay any creditors you choose after you file your petition.

Do I need permission from my spouse to file, and will my husband/wife then become responsible for the bills?

If the two of you were jointly liable on a debt, the non-filing spouse will continue to be responsible for that bill. It usually is necessary for both husband and wife to file if they are jointly responsible for many of their bills.

Is it necessary for husbands and wives to file bankruptcy together?

Husbands and wives are allowed to file together, but whether they do so will depend on a variety of factors that will be evaluated by the attorney. If they file bankruptcy together, only one case filing fee of $175 is required by the court to file the case.

What if I earn a lot of money after I file? Will I have to repay the bills?

No, you won't. The court cannot order you to pay bills out of future income, wages, commissions or profits that you may receive.

What happens if I bought a car financed by a bank, credit union, auto finance company (G.M.A.C., Ford Motor Credit, Chrysler Credit) or other creditor?

You will be able to keep your car. However, you must continue to make the monthly payments on time, and you must sign a reaffirmation agreement, in which you promise to make those payments.

What if I return goods such as furniture, appliances or a car that I owe money on?

Then you will no longer owe any money. This means you have the choice of continuing to pay for goods and keeping them, or returning them and no longer owing the debt.

If You Have A Car Loan

It is important to know about Reaffirmation. If you have an automobile loan and want to keep the car, you have to sign a reaffirmation agreement, agreeing to continue making payments to the creditor.
If you decide to change your mind and surrender the vehicle and get out of the loan, you may do so at any time prior to discharge, or within 60 days after the reaffirmation agreement is filed with the court, whichever occurs later. You must also give notice of the fact that you changed your mind to the creditor and the court.

Will I be able to keep such items as clothes, records, books, kitchenware, bedding, linen and similar items I have bought on credit but will not be paying for because bankruptcy has discharged my debt?

Yes. Only items that have monetary value are of interest to creditors. Because the above items have little or no value, they are of no interest to your creditors. These items are also exempt according to New York State law.

What kinds of bills are discharged in bankruptcy?

These bills will be discharged:

- Medical bills, including hospital and doctor fees.
- Back rent, telephone and utility charges that are in arrears.
- Bank, credit union, signature loans, veterans assistance loans and finance company loans.
- Revolving credit such as MasterCard, Visa, American Express and oil company credit cards.
- Attorneys, legal and court fees.
- Overdrafts or deficiency balances on bank accounts.
- Record or book clubs.
- Storage fees, leases and rentals.
- Most debts owed due to a car accident.
- Most business debts.

Are there any time limits on the bills I want to have discharged?

You can include bills you have not paid for five, 10 or more years, and those that are only a week old. However, if you have incurred a large bill shortly before filing, that bill might not be discharged. This rule usually applies to a consumer debt of more than $1,000 owed for a luxury item to a single creditor for purchases made within 60 days of filing, or for cash advances of more than $1,000, which have been incurred within 60 days of filing.

Do I ever have to repay the bills I list on my bankruptcy petition?

No, unless you choose to do so.

Can I file if I'm married, divorced, separated, in the middle of a divorce, widowed, unemployed, employed, on welfare or if I am not a citizen?

Yes. Your civil status has no bearing on filing bankruptcy.

Can I buy a home, change jobs, start a business, buy furniture or a car, or move to another city or state after I file bankruptcy?

Yes. Bankruptcy does not bar you from your normal daily activities, your civil liberties or rights.

May I file if I have debts in another city or state?

Yes.

Can I file on any amount, and do I have to know the exact amount I owe each creditor?

You can file on any amount; bankruptcy is intended to discharge any amount of debt. But you don't have to know the exact amounts. You can estimate.

Will I lose all my property if I file bankruptcy?

No. If the exemptions are properly taken on your bankruptcy petition, it would be unusual for you to lose any property.

Is it difficult to find a competent lawyer to handle a bankruptcy case?

It depends. In metropolitan areas there usually are some attorneys who concentrate on handling bankruptcy and Chapter 13 cases. It may take a little effort to contact one of these attorneys, but it is worthwhile to find someone who is familiar with the complex workings of the Bankruptcy Code (see Chapter 18).

Is there any alternative to filing bankruptcy?

Yes. You can file a debt consolidation plan under Chapter 13. A large proportion of those who file bankruptcy could pay all or some of their bills through Chapter 13 if they knew more about it. Unfortunately, only a few attorneys are familiar with this proceeding and, therefore, many don't consider it as an alternative to Chapter 7.

How soon after I file Chapter 7 bankruptcy can I file Chapter 7 again?

Six years.

What would the advantages be if I chose Chapter 7?

You would discharge most of your debts, and be able to start again without a deficit budget.

- All collection and garnishment attempts would stop.
- If money problems had been seriously affecting your psychological well-being or your marriage, these problems may be relieved by filing a bankruptcy petition.
- You can usually choose before you file what property will be exempt, and therefore what you will keep.
- You can fulfill any ethical or moral obligation you feel by voluntarily repaying or making a partial repayment to anyone after your debts are discharged or by reaffirming that debt.

5

Chapter 13: The Wage Earner's Plan

Dick Roberts called me up in a panic, four days before his house was to be sold at a foreclosure sale. He wanted to file Chapter 13, pay back at least part of his debts and save the house. He was so upset that I had to spend time reassuring him that a bankruptcy filing would not mean the end of the world.

"Look at it this way, Dick," I said. "You're doing something positive about your financial situation before it gets out of hand.

"You're not poor—you're just broke."

Chapter 13, which is also called the Wage Earner's Plan, is a proceeding designed for individuals with regular income who want to pay their debts but can't. The primary benefit of Chapter 13 is that it allows debtors to pay off part or all of their debts over a longer period of time than is provided for under the original loan contract. During the Chapter 13 plan, which may last three to five years, creditors cannot start or continue collection efforts.

Under a Chapter 13 plan, your debts are not discharged in the same way they are under a Chapter 7 bankruptcy. You formulate a plan of repayment that is confirmed by a court order. Under this plan you pay back what you can afford, which is usually less than 100 percent of the debt you owe. You must have some form of regular income to file Chapter 13. This can come from wages, self-employment, pensions or benefits.

Your debts are placed in the hands of a trustee who acts as a disbursing agent, collecting the money from you and making regular payments to your creditors. These payments may be only 10 or 20 percent of what you originally contracted to pay, and are spread out over three to five years.

Exactly how does Chapter 13 work?

A Chapter 13 plan permits individuals who have a steady source of income to pay part or all of their debts under protection of the bankruptcy court. If you file Chapter 13, you file a petition and a plan with the bankruptcy court. The bankruptcy law requires that the payments you make through the plan to unsecured creditors have a value of at least what the creditors would have received if you had chosen to file a Chapter 7 case.

Relief under Chapter 13 is only allowed to those individuals or small businesses (such as a sole proprietorship, not a corporation), that have less than $250,000 in unsecured debt (this debt could include store charges, loans, credit cards and doctor bills) and less than $750,000 in secured debts (such as car loans, mortgages, etc.). Anyone with greater debts usually must file either Chapter 7 or Chapter 11 of the Bankruptcy Code.

In a typical case, the Witherspoons came into my office, behind on their mortgage by several months, behind on their taxes, and the bank was threatening to foreclose on their house. They owned an automobile and were two months behind on the auto loan, and also owed on unsecured credit cards and hospital bills. Their car was worth only $5,000, but they owed $10,000 on the car loan.

I examined their assets and liabilities, and income and expenses, and came up with a Chapter 13 plan to help them with their debts and prevent foreclosure on their home:

Fair market value of the car......	$ 5,000 + 9% interest
Mortgage arrears	$ 3,000 + 9% interest
Real estate tax arrears	$ 1,000 + 9% interest
Unsecured debt (5% repayment.. on $10,000, miscellaneous unsecured debt such as credit card debt, medical bills)	$ 500
Trustee (7.5%) commission	$ 712
Total:	$10,212 + interest as set forth above
Payments to be paid............ over 60 months	$ 210 per month

Under a Chapter 13 plan, the court allows you to pay back only the fair market value of your vehicle, rather than what you actually owe on the loan. In the Witherspoons' case, this saved them $5,000. They were able to eliminate other unsecured debt that they owed.

Court concerns

The court will look at several factors in deciding whether to approve your Chapter 13 plan. You must include some payment to unsecured creditors, and you must have enough income to make those payments and still cover your living expenses. You must also be able to commit to the plan for the next three to five years.

The court also wants to know that your plan is being filed in good faith. It is not considered bad faith to pay substantially less than 100 percent of your unsecured debt (credit card charges, doctor bills, etc.).

However, the court will not look kindly on, or consider as good faith, a plan that does not include the spouse's income or a plan where most of the debt was rooted in criminal conduct.

What happens in a Chapter 13 case

A Chapter 13 case begins with the filing of the official forms showing assets and liabilities, property you are claiming as exempt, your income, expenses, statement of affairs and your plan.

You and your attorney will have to work out a budget, which will determine the total amount of your monthly expenses. The difference between your monthly expenses and your income is the money used to repay your creditors.

You and your attorney will have to work out a budget

In order to complete the forms that make up the petition and schedules, you will have to provide this information:

- A list of all of your creditors.

- The source, amount, frequency and reliability of your income.

- A list of all your property.

- A detailed list of your monthly living expenses, including food, clothing, shelter, utilities, taxes, transportation, medicine and any other bills you may have.

Your creditors don't have to approve the plan. The court will do this regardless of your creditors' views — in most instances — if you fulfill the requirements set forth in the Bankruptcy Code.

I had one man come in, just married, who had gone $20,000 into debt with credit cards. He and his wife weren't sure they were going to file, but soon after their first appointment with me, they began to get a number of harassing phone calls from creditors.

Instead of walking a tightrope every day, worrying about their bills and how to avoid these harassing phone calls, they chose to file a Chapter 13 plan whereby they paid back 10 cents on every dollar they owed. After filing they were relieved to be free of their creditors.

What are the advantages of filing Chapter 13?

There are many significant advantages to selecting Chapter 13.

1. As a general rule you are able to keep all your assets and property as long as you make your payments to the Chapter 13 trustee as agreed. You protect non-exempt assets by filing Chapter 13.

2. There are great benefits to Chapter 13 relative to how secured claims are handled. Let's say you have an unpaid balance on your car loan of $10,000, but the car has a value of only $6,000. In that case, the court might approve the "cram down" of the loan to $6,000 as a secured claim, with your monthly payments being reduced to $100 per month plus a small amount of interest. The balance of the loan might be forgiven as part of the Chapter 13 plan.

   If you decide you don't want the car any longer, your Chapter 13 plan might provide that you turn the car over to the secured creditor (who has a lien against the car) and perhaps you may get out of the balance by virtue of the Chapter 13 case.

   This example is not limited to just automobile loans. It may be applied to any secured loan other than most mortgages.

3. Let's suppose you have fallen behind on your mortgage payments and the bank has written a letter indicating they might start a foreclosure action. Or, the situation is worse. Let's say you have actually received foreclosure papers. This is certainly a situation no one likes to get into. However, Chapter 13 may help solve your problem.

   For example, you have $9,000 in delinquent mortgage payments. You can propose to pay the $9,000 in arrearages through the Chapter 13 plan at $150 per month over 5 years with a small amount of interest. If you can afford to do this, a Chapter 13 plan may be approved for you. While you can put the accumulated past due mortgage payments under the Chapter 13 plan, you must resume making your future, monthly payments on your home mortgage loan on time (referred to as post-petition mortgage payments).

4. If you file Chapter 13 and you had people co-sign any of your loans, your creditors are not permitted to collect from these co-signers as long as your Chapter 13 plan provides that the co-signed loans will be paid in full. Perhaps the co-signed loan you have requires a payment of $200 per month for 12 months. Chapter 13 would allow you to modify that arrangement and reduce the payment to a much lower amount where it may be paid back over five years through your plan.

5. The discharge you receive under Chapter 13 is much broader than what you receive under Chapter 7. When you complete your Chapter 13 plan, creditors cannot require you to pay them in full, even if you used fraudulent means to get credit or filed a false financial statement.

6. A Chapter 7 case may only be filed every six years. However, Chapter 13 allows you to file more often. Chapter 13 may be filed repeatedly, although each time you file it will appear on your credit record. In addition, each filing must be proposed in good faith; otherwise your plan may not be confirmed by the court.

7. Another potential advantage to filing Chapter 13 involves your credit. The Chapter 13 will remain on your credit record for six years and nine months, whereas the Chapter 7 will remain on your credit record for nine years and nine months. Some potential creditors might prefer that you file a Chapter 13 over Chapter 7.

8. Certain debts, such as most taxes, are considered priority and must be paid in full. Chapter 13 will stop a real estate tax foreclosure — it will also stop the IRS or the State of New York from taking your property or garnishing your paycheck.

So for example, if the IRS demands full payment on the $3,000 of back taxes you owe, you may file Chapter 13 and pay this back at the rate of $50.00 per month. In many instances, no interest is required. In some instances, this tax debt may be eliminated by paying only a small percentage on the dollar (see Chapter 16 of this book on taxes).

Summary

You may want to consider a Chapter 13 plan if you are experiencing any of these situations:

1. You have a substantial amount of debt and do not have the ability to repay in a timely fashion.
2. Your auto has depreciated in value and you owe more on it than what it is worth.
3. You have a high monthly payment on your auto loan. You can lower the payment and stretch it out over 60 months.
4. You have fallen behind on your mortgage, but would like to catch up the back payments and keep your home.
5. You have fallen behind on taxes.
6. You own non-exempt assets that might be lost if Chapter 7 is filed.
7. You are not eligible to file Chapter 7 because you previously filed Chapter 7 within the past six years.
8. You are not eligible to file Chapter 7 because you filed Chapter 13 within the past six years, your Chapter 13 plan was completed, and you repaid your creditors less than 70 percent.
9. You want to pay your creditors as much as your budget will allow.

Check out the examples of Chapter 13 plans in the appendix, look at your finances, and consult a lawyer to determine if Chapter 13 is the best option for you. Many clients find that a Chapter 13 plan gives them an opportunity to correct what may seem a hopeless situation.

6

Going Through Chapter 13: Step-by-Step

One day I was working through a Chapter 13 plan with Sally Jones, who seemed unusually jittery for someone who had already made a decision about how to solve her debt problems. Sally kept looking at her watch and shifting her weight around in her chair.

"Sally," I said, "is something bothering you? You seem awfully nervous today."

"Well I'm just wondering how long this will take," she said. "I left my daughter waiting in my car downstairs. It's double-parked, and as a matter of fact, she's just about to have a baby and she's waiting for me to take her to the hospital."

Needless to say, we finished up the appointment rather quickly.

After you have met with your attorney and discussed the options available to you, you will begin the following process if you decide to proceed with filing Chapter 13:

Step 1: Meet with your attorney, who takes information to process your Chapter 13 petition.

Step 2: At the first or second conference you are asked to pay part of the legal fee and disbursements, and your attorney completes the Chapter 13 petition. The court is required to charge a filing fee. At the time of this writing, that filing fee is $160. The bulk of the legal fee can be paid through the plan.

Step 3: Your Chapter 13 petition is typed.

Step 4: You return to the office for your third conference, to review and sign the Chapter 13 petition.

Step 5: Your petition is filed with the bankruptcy court and a filing fee is paid to the court. Your petition includes a detailed list of your debts, all of your assets and the exemptions you claim. The bankruptcy court assigns your file a case number, and the automatic stay (which prevents your creditors from harassing you) takes effect. When your petition is filed, a trustee also is appointed by the court. This trustee will administer the case.

Creditors, by law, generally cannot initiate or continue any lawsuits, wage garnishment or even telephone calls demanding payment after your petition has been filed. They are notified by the trustee's office that you have filed a Chapter 13 petition.

Step 6: You can file your plan of repayment with your petition, or you can file it within 15 days of filing your petition. Plans, which must be approved by the court, provide for payments of fixed amounts to the trustee on a regular basis.

Step 7: You receive a copy of your petition in the mail. You should examine it for accuracy and keep it for your records.

Step 8: Within 30 days after your plan has been filed, even if it has not yet been approved by the court, your payments to the trustee must begin.

Step 9: A 341 Meeting (the meeting of your creditors) and a confirmation hearing are scheduled to take place within 20 to 40 days after your case is filed. Your creditors are notified of the meeting, which you are required to attend. This may be the only time you have to appear at a hearing.

The primary reason for the 341 Meeting and the confirmation hearing is to allow the Chapter 13 trustee and the judge an opportunity to question the debtor under oath regarding various aspects of the Chapter 13 case. The trustee and the judge need to make sure that the plan filed complies with various provisions of the Bankruptcy Code.

Your actual involvement may be five to 10 minutes. However, there are often many cases scheduled and you may be required to wait anywhere from 30 minutes to two hours before your case is called and heard first by the trustee and then by the judge.

Step 10: Typical questions asked at the 341 Meeting by the trustee include:

- Did you list all of your assets?
- Did you list all of your creditors?

If you own real estate, the following questions might be asked:

- How did you arrive at the home's value?

- What is the mortgage balance?

- If there are mortgage arrearages, do you understand those are normally paid through the Chapter 13 plan?

- Do you understand that all future post-petition mortgage and future post-petition tax payments are made by the debtor directly outside of the plan, and must be made in a timely fashion?

Do you own any motor vehicles?
If yes, these additional questions will be asked:

- May I see a copy of your title?

- Is there anything wrong with the motor vehicle?

- What is the mileage on the odometer?

- What are the year and make of the car?

- Will you please show me proof of collision insurance?

- The trustee will look in the NADA auto value book and set a price for the value of the motor vehicle. The trustee will then ask if you think the price he has set is fair.

Additional questions will be asked depending on the case. To give you a general idea, these additional questions may be asked:

- Do you own any hunting or sports equipment?

- Do you have any lawsuits pending against anyone?

- Do you own any valuable collections?

The trustee will then review the plan being proposed and discuss the percentage being offered to unsecured creditors.

- If you are offering your creditors only partial payment of your total debt, you must commit all of your expected disposable income over 36 months. Disposable income is defined as the income not reasonably necessary to maintain or support you and your family. Your plan must provide for payments of fixed amounts to the trustee on a regular basis, usually weekly, biweekly or monthly.

Also, the amount to be paid to priority creditors (taxes or child support) will be discussed along with these other items:

- What the car creditor will receive.
- What the payment to the trustee will be.
- How long the plan will last.
- Did your payments begin yet?

Finally, the trustee will ask if you understand the plan.

How does the proposed plan work?

If you file Chapter 13, your payments must constitute all of your disposable income for a 36-month period. When we prepare the plan, we look at the total income the family has available, and from that we subtract your regular monthly expenses for the family, such as rent, food, clothing, auto insurance, etc. Whatever is left over after all the regular family expenses are paid is what you generally pay to the Chapter 13 trustee.

The Chapter 13 plan is filed at the court, and is reviewed by the Chapter 13 trustee assigned to your case. It is the trustee's duty to verify the accuracy and reasonableness of the plan, and to distribute the money to your creditors. You must begin making payments to the trustee within 30 days of the date your case is filed. You often begin making your payments to your trustee even before you appear in court where your case is approved. You will receive a Chapter 13 discharge after all the payments provided for by the plan are made.

The Chapter 13 plan normally reduces the amount you pay to your creditors and also extends your time to repay certain debts that must often be paid anyway. The repayment period usually lasts for three years. However, if circumstances require, the plan can last for up to five years.

There are significant benefits to clients who file Chapter 13, and these plans most often result in the client paying significantly less to the creditors than what is actually due.

Step 11: The Confirmation Hearing

Anywhere from five to 60 minutes following the 341 Meeting (the meeting the trustee conducts), you appear before the bankruptcy judge for the confirmation hearing. The purpose of the confirmation hearing is to enable the judge to inquire into various aspects of the case. The judge must decide if the Chapter 13 plan complies with all requirements of the Bankruptcy Code; and he must do this before the plan can be confirmed.

What questions are asked by the bankruptcy judge at the confirmation hearing? Each judge has his own style and has a great deal of discretion as to what he or she may ask. The type of questions to be asked will also depend upon the unique facts of the case. The following are some of the most common questions the judge may ask after you are sworn in. Many were previously asked by the trustee at the 341 Meeting:

- What are your name and address?

If you own real estate, the following may be covered:

- How do you arrive at the value?

- When did you buy the home?

- Have you made significant improvements to the property?

- If there are mortgage arrearages, do you understand the Chapter 13 plan covers the arrearages, but all post-petition mortgage payments must be paid by you directly and on time?

- Your motor vehicle is valued at _____ dollars. Is that a fair value?

- Are you employed?

- Where are you employed?

- Is your employment stable?

- Do you work for the same employer that you told your attorney about when he prepared your Chapter 13 petition?

- Do you understand your plan requires you to pay to the trustee _____ dollars per month for _____ months?

- Can you afford the plan payments and still make ends meet at home?

If you are collecting unemployment insurance, the following may be asked:

- Can you afford the plan payments?
- When will you get back to work?
- How is your job search going?

If you receive support or alimony, the following may be asked:

- How long will you continue to receive it?
- Is it guaranteed?
- How much do you get per month?

If your Chapter 13 plan is feasible, meets the best interest of creditors test and complies with all aspects of the Bankruptcy Code, the judge will immediately confirm the plan.

Occasionally, a creditor objects to the plan on technical grounds, or the judge requires additional information and will not confirm the plan at the first confirmation hearing. If this happens, do not be alarmed. In most cases, your attorney will resolve the creditor's dispute, or will provide the judge with whatever is required, and the plan will be confirmed at a later date; usually within 30 days following the confirmation hearing.

Step 12: Within 30 days after your plan has been filed, even if it has not yet been approved by the court, you must begin making payments to the trustee. If the plan is confirmed by the judge, the trustee begins to make payments to your creditors from the money he or she has received from you. Your payments to the trustee are automatically deducted from your paycheck for the length of your plan. If you are self-employed or your income is from other sources, you can make other arrangements for payment with the trustee. The trustee distributes the funds to creditors according to the terms of your plan.

Step 13: If you live up to your promise and fulfill all of your payments in the plan, you receive a discharge. Because you have kept your promise, the judge formally forgives any remaining balance due on debts covered by your plan, except for most taxes, most student loans, family support obligations and fines.

Once your plan has been confirmed, it is your responsibility to make sure it succeeds. You must make your regular payments to the trustee, which means you are going to have to live on a fixed budget for a long period of time. You will be able to keep the property you own, but you cannot take on any significant debts without first obtaining approval. This is because any further debt load could endanger your ability to fulfill the plan.

Making Payments On Time
Through Automatic Wage Deductions

By having the plan payments automatically deducted from your paycheck, it is likely that your payments will be made on time and your plan will be successfully completed. If, for some reason, you do not make your payments, your case could be dismissed or it may be converted to a liquidation proceeding under Chapter 7 of the Bankruptcy Code. Statistics indicate that plans where a wage order is in effect have a much better chance of completion. It is strongly recommended that you consent to the wage order.

7

Important Facts About Chapter 13

Your case number and Chapter 13 petition

A copy of your Chapter 13 petition, which will have your case number on it, will be sent to you by your attorney. This is an important document and it should be kept in a safe, handy place. You'll need to refer to it whenever you contact your attorney, the bankruptcy court or your Chapter 13 trustee.

The 341 Meeting and Confirmation Hearing

Residents of Monroe, Ontario, Livingston, Wayne, Seneca and Yates counties will attend court at 100 State St., Rochester. For residents of Steuben, Schuyler, Orleans, Genesee, Wyoming or Chemung counties, the meeting is held at Schuyler County Courthouse, N. Franklin St., Watkins Glen. Others will be notified by their attorney and the Chapter 13 trustee as to the location of this appearance.

Making those payments

In order to avoid having your case dismissed by the court, you must begin to make payments to the trustee within one month of the date you filed your petition. You must also continue to make these payments on time.

This is relatively simple for those who are employed, because most Chapter 13 payments are made through a payroll deduction with the debtor's place of employment.

In unusual cases (self-employment, sole proprietorships), or if you receive Social Security, unemployment, etc., payments can be made by money order, cashier's check or personal check, which must include your name, address and Chapter 13 case number. Never mail cash. Payments can be made by mail or in person between 9 a.m. and 4:30 p.m. at the Chapter 13 office, 3136 S. Winton Rd., Suite 206, Rochester, NY 14623. Checks should be made payable to George M. Reiber, Trustee. Any changes in employment or address must be reported in writing to your attorney's office as well as to the Chapter 13 trustee.

Court's jurisdiction of wage order

You and your employer should understand that the wage order issued by the court is not an attachment or garnishment. An attachment or garnishment can come only from someone to whom you owe money, and you do not owe the court any money.

The court is simply carrying out its duty to administer the plan you voluntarily filed, and in which you voluntarily gave the court exclusive jurisdiction over your future pay during the course of your plan.

Many employers think more highly of the employee who pays his or her delinquent bills through Chapter 13.

If you do have problems with your credit union . . .

Occasionally, when a credit union is involved in the Chapter 13 plan, this lender will exert pressure on the borrower. This leads the employee to believe his or her job may be in jeopardy. This is illegal in that it constitutes an attempt to obtain creditor preferences. Any such actions must be reported to your attorney immediately.

Contacts by creditors

Some creditors are large institutions whose billing is handled on large computer systems. In these cases it may take several weeks before the proper department is advised of your Chapter 13 petition. First, check the petition to be certain the creditor is listed and the address is correct. Then simply send any bills, letters or other communications back to the creditor with a notation of your Chapter 13 case number and the date it was filed. If the creditor still continues to bill you, contact your attorney.

If you are contacted by phone or in person, tell the representative about your Chapter 13 plan, give him the name and address of your attorney, and get the party's name. Then report the contact, and the name of the person who made the contact, to your attorney.

Never give a creditor any information other than the number of your Chapter 13 case, the date it was filed and the name of your attorney or paralegal.

Balance due creditors

In Chapter 13 you cannot pick and choose which creditors you will pay off, or save one to pay on the side. All creditors must be paid by the trustee and under the terms of the law (with the exception of real estate debts — see pg. 37).

You will receive a Report of Receipts and Disbursements from the trustee every six months, in November and May. This computerized record shows all payments received by the trustee and to whom the money was sent. It will also show you how much you still owe your creditors and how much time is left on your plan.

Claims of creditors

In order for your creditors to be paid through your plan, they must file a "proof of claim." Most creditors must file their claims within 90 days of the first date set for your meeting of creditors. Claims of a governmental unit are deemed timely filed, if filed within 180 days after the bankruptcy petition is filed.

After your plan has been in operation for several months, the trustee will send you a list of everyone who has filed a claim in your plan, called the "motion to allow claims." The trustee can pay only those claims that are filed and approved. Any others will not be paid and will be discharged (forgiven), with the exception of certain taxes, secured claims, child support, student loans and tuition.

Carefully review the motion to allow claims and your trustee's Report of Receipts and Disbursements, mailed to you twice each year. If a creditor is not listed, is listed incorrectly, or if any amount claimed appears incorrect, contact the Chapter 13 office and your attorney's office in writing.

Amendments to add creditors

Include all your creditors on the forms you submit to your lawyer. If you fail to include a creditor and your lawyer's office has to prepare amended or additional schedules, there may be an additional charge.

Amendments to add creditors must be served within 90 days of the date of your meeting with the creditors, or the amendment will not be permitted. If the amendment is late, you will have to pay this debt.

How creditors are paid

The money you pay to the Chapter 13 trustee is used to pay all expenses, including your attorney and creditors. Creditors are paid according to the type of claim: priority, secured or unsecured. Generally, delinquent child support, delinquent alimony, taxes (which are priority) and secured claims are paid first, and unsecured claims are paid after the others have been paid in full. For this reason, it can be several months or even years before the first payments are made to unsecured creditors.

Permission for credit

With the exception of emergency medical or hospital care, a debtor in a Chapter 13 plan cannot incur any new debt over $500 without prior approval of the Chapter 13 trustee. If you find you must replace some necessary articles by using credit, you should contact your attorney.

Requesting Permission To Borrow

Do not contact the trustee's office directly requesting permission to borrow. Many of our clients have contacted the trustee directly. Clients think that since their income increased, borrowing would be allowed. In several instances the client received an unexpected response:

1. *borrowing denied,*

2. *since income had increased, the trustee wanted a much larger dividend to unsecured creditors.*

Let your attorney review your situation. Your attorney can make a borrowing request on your behalf if it is appropriate.

Obtaining credit without permission

To obtain credit without permission is a violation of the Confirmation Order and places your plan in serious jeopardy.

Automobile insurance

If you are financing a car, it is important to have collision insurance and to name the bank or lender as the loss-payee. This protects the lender in the event of an accident. Your attorney may ask for proof of collision insurance when preparing your plan. You should bring proof of collision insurance into court when you have your 341 Meeting.

Real estate debts

Any debts you owe that are secured by a mortgage — on real estate or a contract for a mobile home — are usually paid directly by you. These payments are included in your budget when your plan is set up. Remember, failure to make mortgage or trailer payments on a timely basis will result in the loss of your home, and the court will allow the mortgage company to proceed with foreclosure.

Utilities

Utility bills incurred after your petition is filed are your responsibility and should be paid on time. If you list a utility company on your Chapter 13 petition, it cannot refuse you service, but it may require a security deposit, which you usually can arrange to pay in installments (see Appendix B).

Checking out checks

Writing a bad check is a criminal matter, and a creditor who holds a bad check can either join your Chapter 13 plan or prosecute the transaction as a crime. The filing of a Chapter 13 case does not stop criminal prosecution for a bad check.

Bank accounts

Any salary, wages or commissions you earn after your Chapter 13 petition has been filed belong to you. You are free to open a bank account or checking account after the petition is filed.

Requests for dismissal by debtor

Federal bankruptcy law allows you to have your Chapter 13 case dismissed at any time by contacting your lawyer and putting the request in writing. You should understand, however, that dismissing your case reactivates all unpaid or disputed debts, all interest, all finance charges that are not allowed by the court, and all debts to creditors who did not file their claims.

In addition, you will have to deal with those creditors on their terms.

The Chapter 13 discharge

When you have successfully completed your Chapter 13 plan, you'll receive a "discharge." The discharge states that you are not obligated to pay any unsecured debts that were included in the plan, but were not paid in full through the plan.

For example: If you offer to pay 10 cents on the dollar to your unsecured creditors (credit card and medical bills), the remaining 90 cents on the dollar will be discharged.

Unsecured debts are defined as obligations based only on your future ability to pay.

Bankruptcy law regarding Chapter 13 is complex, and you should consult a lawyer before you file Chapter 13. Certain debts cannot be discharged, including alimony and support obligations, some student loans, certain taxes, secured obligations and fines. All other debts, including some that cannot be discharged in a Chapter 7 filing (such as those incurred by fraud, embezzlement, larceny, willful, malicious injury and some taxes), are dischargeable under Chapter 13.

In effect, in return for your willingness to undergo the discipline of a three- to five-year repayment plan, a broader discharge is provided than is available under a Chapter 7 bankruptcy.

Hardship discharge

Occasionally, after a person has confirmed a plan, circumstances will arise that will keep him from completing it. The person may become ill or disabled, or be unable to work for some other reason.

In these cases, the debtor can ask the court to grant a "hardship discharge." Generally, this is available only to those who cannot complete their plan because of circumstances beyond their control and through no fault of their own. Modification of the plan must not be possible, and creditors must already have received at least as much in repayment as they would have received under a Chapter 7 liquidation proceeding.

8

Questions And Concerns About Chapter 13

Many people experience a great sense of relief after they file bankruptcy. After the Bloomingfields filed Chapter 13, Mrs. Bloomingfield called me on the phone:

"Jeffrey, you can't imagine the total peace of mind we feel now that we've gone through Chapter 13. We feel that our lives are starting all over again!

"I don't feel afraid anymore to answer my phone, because I know bill collectors won't be on the other end. It's hard to believe — at one point not too long ago, our lives were crushed financially."

I hear stories like this over and over again. Instead of feeling depressed, embarrassed and burdened with debt, most people feel uplifted when they file bankruptcy.

Who can file a Chapter 13 plan?

Only an individual or a married couple, not a corporation or partnership, can file a Chapter 13. There are also limitations on the amount of debt you can have. Anyone with secured debts that are more than $750,000 or unsecured debts more than $250,000 cannot use Chapter 13. Those with larger debts must use Chapter 11 if they want to avoid Chapter 7.

Must you be employed to use a Chapter 13 plan?

Generally, yes, but if you have regular income from self-employment, a pension, Social Security, unemployment insurance, welfare, union benefits, disability insurance, alimony, odd jobs, income from family members, or child support, a Chapter 13 plan still can be used. Many small businesses — those owned by individuals — can file and obtain the benefits of Chapter 13.

Does Chapter 13 get your creditors "off your back?"

Yes. When your attorney files your Chapter 13 petition with the bankruptcy court, a court order immediately takes effect. It will prevent your creditors from harassing you for payment at home and on the job and from contacting friends, relatives or your boss. Your creditors cannot repossess your property (without specific court permission) or garnish your wages. Even the state tax authorities and the Internal Revenue Service cannot bother you.

How are new bills handled after you file Chapter 13?

Chapter 13 mainly deals with your old bills. Your usual living expenses for rent or mortgage, food, clothing, insurance and utilities will come out of your remaining income after your Chapter 13 plan is paid.

Is it true that under Chapter 13 co-signers on consumer debts are also protected?

Yes. Those who co-signed for you on various loans or purchases will not be affected by your Chapter 13 plan as long as you pay 100 percent of the debt they have co-signed, including interest required in the loan agreement. If not, creditors can approach co-signers for the balance of the debt immediately. Keep in mind that you can choose to pay 100 percent of a co-signed debt, yet pay only a small portion of your other debts.

Is the co-signer's credit record affected? The co-signer's credit record may already be marked slow pay if you were late with payments prior to filing. The Chapter 13 plan may also cause the co-signer's credit record to be marked slow pay.

Can I consolidate all my bills?

Yes, except your post-petition mortgage payments. Unless special circumstances exist, your post-petition mortgage payments will be paid on your own, outside the Chapter 13 plan. Any mortgage payments you missed prior to filing your plan (pre-petition payments) will be included in the plan.

Can my creditors stop me from filing a Chapter 13 plan?

No, creditors cannot stop you from exercising your right to file under Chapter 13. Creditors will sometimes tell you they "will not accept the filing" or they "will prevent the court from accepting the filing." Don't believe these statements. Let your lawyer or paralegal advise you how your plan will work.

How long does a Chapter 13 plan last?

The usual time frame is 36 months. However, you can pay off your plan sooner if you wish, and with special court permission you can extend your plan for 48 to 60 months.

What are the usual costs involved in filing a non-business Chapter 13?

Costs, including disbursements, may vary depending on your case. The attorney's fee and disbursements must be approved by the court. In many cases a substantial part of the fee and disbursements can be included in the plan with the rest of your bills. If your case is more complex or involves a business, a higher fee will be required.

Is it true that if you filed bankruptcy in the past six years, you can still file a Chapter 13 plan?

Yes. You cannot file a second bankruptcy (Chapter 7) within six years of the first, but you can file a Chapter 13.

What happens to my Chapter 13 plan if I cannot work for a while because I am ill, injured or have lost my job?

The court and the Chapter 13 trustee will give you an opportunity to explain your situation and will keep your Chapter 13 plan in place if your disability is temporary or your lack of work is not too prolonged.

Are there any court hearings?

Yes. About one month after you file, you will have to appear in court. At this time the Chapter 13 trustee and the judge will ask you several questions, and your attorney will ask the court to approve your Chapter 13 plan.

Do I need permission from my spouse to file?

No. Any person who is employed or has a regular income can file at any time.

To whom will I make my Chapter 13 payments?

Usually payments are deducted from your paycheck and sent to the office of the Chapter 13 trustee for distribution to your creditors.

Will the court take any of my property?

No. Chapter 13 allows you to keep all property, including your home, furniture, savings, car, jewelry and household goods.

May I file Chapter 13 if I am self-employed or own a small business?

Yes. The Bankruptcy Code allows for those who are self-employed and those who are in a sole proprietorship with less than $250,000 in unsecured debt and $750,000 in secured debt to file Chapter 13.

Who will notify my creditors of my Chapter 13 filing?

The Chapter 13 trustee notifies all creditors.

If I have been sued, am behind in my bills, have debts in a collection agency, have had my wages attached, have a judgment against me, a house in foreclosure or other legal problems, can I still file Chapter 13 and stop these actions?

Yes, Chapter 13 stops almost all types of court actions.

Will Chapter 13 stop mortgage foreclosures, late charges and added interest on past-due bills?

Generally speaking, yes. If your plan calls for it, the court may approve a plan in which you are given an extension period to catch up on back payments on your mortgage.

How about credit union payments that are being deducted from my paycheck?

The credit union will be required to stop deducting money from your paycheck.

What will happen to the garnishment that is currently being taken from my wages?

This will be stopped within a short time after your petition has been filed.

Must I list credit cards or charge accounts I do not owe money on?

No.

Can I file if my income is from SSI, Social Security, disability, veterans assistance or other monetary assistance?

As long as these payments allow you to pay rent, food and other necessities of life together with your Chapter 13 payment, your petition will probably be approved by the court.

Do I need a co-signer of any kind to file Chapter 13?

No.

What if you are in Chapter 13 and run into additional financial difficulty?

What happens if you can't keep up with your Chapter 13 payments? If you fail to make a substantial number of your payments to the trustee, he will ask the judge to dismiss your case. If the case is dismissed, the collection calls will begin again, and you may have your car, for example, repossessed or your home foreclosed upon. Stay in touch with your attorney and paralegal if you run into problems, they can often suggest a number of solutions that might help you. What we recommend will depend on your circumstances. In some instances you can immediately file a new case once your old 13 plan is dismissed and obtain an additional 36 to 60 months to pay on a new plan. Perhaps Chapter 7 might be an option to consider. Don't panic — call your lawyer or paralegal for a conference to review all your options.

9

Additional Reminders When Filing Bankruptcy

Just like everything else in life, filing bankruptcy or Chapter 13 is not as simple as it looks. There are some things you have to be cautious about in order to protect your property and some of the people in your life. Always be totally honest with your lawyer so that he or she can help you over the rough spots. The following is a list of things you should give some thought if you file Chapter 7 or 13.

Did you have a co-signer?

Before your bankruptcy, you may have bought something on credit or borrowed money and had a friend or relative co-sign for you. That person will still be responsible for that particular debt. If you want to protect your co-signer after you file Chapter 7, you can continue to make payments on the debt. You must be certain, however, to list the person as a creditor on your list of debts.

If it happens that you are filing Chapter 7 and your co-signer is in bad financial shape and wants to file bankruptcy at the same time you do, your attorney, or an attorney of the co-signer's choice, can legally wipe out the debt for both of you.

If you are filing Chapter 13, your co-signer is protected up to the amount of the debt you are repaying through your Chapter 13 plan. However, the creditor can require the co-signer to repay the portion of the debt that you are not paying through your plan.

For instance, if you owe a creditor $5,000 on a loan that a relative or friend co-signed for you, and you plan to pay back all your creditors only 10 percent of your total debts, you plan to pay that creditor only $500. The creditor could legally require your co-signer to pay the remaining $4,500.

To prevent this from happening, you can plan to pay most of your creditors 10 percent of your debt, but ask that your co-signed debt be paid back 100 percent and interest.

Have you inherited money or property?

If you are due an inheritance when you file bankruptcy or if you inherit money or property from someone who has died within six months after you file bankruptcy, you can lose a portion or all of this inheritance to the bankruptcy court. The court will take out enough money to pay the bills listed in your petition, plus a little for court costs. Any remaining funds will be paid to you.

Do you owe money for back rent?

Renters who have not paid the rent on their apartment or house for several months can have the back rent discharged when they file bankruptcy. However, under the law, the landlord has the right to evict you from the residence because he has not received the back rent.

Credit union debts

You may owe one or more debts to a credit union. You can choose to walk away from all of those loans, you can pay them all, or you can pay only the ones you decide to pay. Talk to your lawyer and if you are filing a Chapter 7, he or she will help you handle the credit union in the way you would like.

Creditors you want to pay off

There may be some creditors you would like to pay off after you file a Chapter 7 bankruptcy. It is recommended you make no commitments, verbal or written, until after your hearing in bankruptcy court. Right after the hearing you can talk with your lawyer and discuss the topic of reaffirming.

Under Chapter 13, you cannot choose to pay some creditors and not others, and you can't pay some debts personally, outside your Chapter 13 plan. All creditors must be listed in your petition, and all will be paid by the Chapter 13 trustee. You can, however, have the trustee pay back some creditors in full (for instance, the loans you have had co-signed), and others only partially. Post-petition mortgage payments are paid directly by you, they are not paid by the trustee.

Bankruptcy and divorce

Bankruptcy attorneys often see clients who are separated or in the middle of a divorce. This will not affect your ability to file bankruptcy. But, you should remember that the purpose of bankruptcy is only to keep creditors from bothering you and to get you out of debt.

Divorce proceedings are completely separate from bankruptcy proceedings. The divorce court can order you or your spouse to pay fees for your spouse's lawyer, child support and alimony; bankruptcy does not relieve you of these obligations.

Bonding for employment

Sometimes bankruptcy can be a problem for those who have to be bonded at their job. If you have to be bonded now, or think you might have to be bonded in the future, talk to your employer and to your lawyer about it before you file.

Retirement/profit sharing plans

Usually you cannot take money out of a retirement, company stock plan, company savings or profit sharing plan at work before you retire or quit your job. Therefore, that money cannot be taken by the courts if you file bankruptcy.

There may be certain cases where a pension, stock plan or profit sharing plan may not be exempt and the court could take the funds you have on deposit away from you.

Be sure to talk about the above circumstances with your lawyer when you consider filing Chapter 13 or Chapter 7.

Commission payments

Some people, such as real estate and insurance agents, receive commissions that are paid to them months after the sale has been made. If you expect to receive commissions in the future, be sure to talk to your attorney about it so they will not be lost to the trustee in bankruptcy.

The case of dual debts

If you owe more than one debt to a bank, credit union or finance company, you can discharge one debt through Chapter 7 bankruptcy and continue to pay the other one off if you wish. You must, however, make sure you tell the lender which account you are continuing to pay on when you send in your payments.

Remember that in Chapter 13 all creditors and debts must be listed and treated equally.

Adding creditors

You may forget to list some creditors, or give the wrong address for some, when you sign your bankruptcy papers. You can add creditors and correct addresses later, but this takes extra time and work by your attorney. Please note that your lawyer may have to charge you extra for this work, and that the amount depends on how much has to be done.

There are also very strict time limits for adding creditors to your petition. You must let your attorney know as soon as possible if you want to make additions. If the omitted creditor is not properly listed before the deadline, you may have to pay the debt in full.

Electric, gas, telephone and water bills

When you owe money to utility companies and list them in your bankruptcy, the overdue bills will be discharged. The utility company cannot refuse to serve you in the future.

The utility may ask you for a security deposit. This is usually an average of two or three months of your balanced billing, or two or three months of your highest bills during the year. It can be paid off in monthly increments over a few months. (Check with your local utility companies' customer service departments for up-to-date information, or see Appendix B.)

If you have been in business and the business owes a large bill, you will not lose service at your house. You may have to pay the security deposit on your home service.

Many clients don't want to pay a large security deposit, so they choose to pay off the utility bill before signing their bankruptcy papers. This way the utility is not notified of the bankruptcy and the deposit is not required.

When you owe money to utility companies and list them in your bankruptcy, the overdue bills will be discharged

Taxes are certain

In a Chapter 7 bankruptcy, unpaid taxes may be paid out of the estate – if there is an asset estate. Usually the Internal Revenue Service and the State of New York will file a claim for your unpaid taxes. If they do not, it is best that you and your attorney file one for them.

If there is no claim filed for back taxes, the taxing agency can come to you later and demand you pay the claim personally.

If you want a claim filed, you must bring your tax bill or other information about your tax debt into your attorney's office. Because you may not know if the IRS or the state has filed a claim until after your first court meeting, we suggest you plan to see your attorney after that meeting. Be ready to file any necessary tax claims at that time. There may be an additional charge to file these claims.

For more information on taxes, see Chapter 16.

When you have money in the bank

You must bring to your attorney's attention information with respect to your bank accounts. The attorney needs to know the name of the bank and the balance in the account on the date the case will be filed. This includes checking and savings accounts, CD's, brokerage accounts and credit union accounts.

The attorney also needs to know if your name is on the account of another. For example, you may have your name on an elderly parent's account or on a child's account. If the funds belong to another, let your attorney know.

Close Accounts When
You Owe The Bank Money

If you have money in a bank and you also owe that same bank money, upon notice of the Chapter 7 or Chapter 13 filing, they may freeze your account and eventually take your money. It is important that you close all accounts before filing when you owe that same bank money. If you wrote checks in an account, let the checks clear and close the account before the case is filed. You can have a bank account or checking account, but not at a bank you owe money to. Let your lawyer know about all your accounts before your case is filed. Your attorney wants to protect your money, but to do that he or she has to know about it.

Credit unions

Where credit unions are concerned, names can be deceiving. Often, your credit union may carry the name of your employer or of your union. Neither the company nor the union, however, owns the credit union. Each credit union is owned by its members.

Members buy shares in credit unions and in return are entitled, subject to an approved credit application, to borrow money from the credit union. Usually, interest rates at credit unions are lower than those at banks or other lending institutions. The drawback is that usually the credit union wants a higher payment, and a payment each time the employee is paid, so that the loan is paid back faster. This can make it difficult to make payments on your other debts.

Gambling losses

The Bankruptcy Code requires people to keep good records of all of their finances, including gambling wins and losses. Many people, however, do not keep any record of their gambling money.

If you have lost large sums of money gambling, and don't have any record of this, it is possible the trustee or one of your creditors will object to the discharge of your debts. Unless you can convince the judge you did lose the money, and can produce good records to prove it, you may not be able to get a discharge in bankruptcy.

Owning a home and filing Chapter 7 or 13

If you own a home, we might advise you to get an accurate appraisal and be able to tell the court just how much it is worth. A valuation that is either too high or too low can cause problems.

For example, if you say the house is worth $45,000 and you owe $35,000 against it, your equity is $10,000. If, however, the court determines your house is really worth $55,000, you can be required to pay the difference into the estate.

In the above example, the judge could ask the homeowner to pay the trustee $10,000.

The law gives an individual a $10,000 homestead exemption for the equity in the home; a couple gets a $20,000 exemption if the home is jointly owned. Under the Bankruptcy Code, this equity cannot be touched by the trustee or creditors.

When you bought your home, did you get a new mortgage or did you assume the seller's mortgage? If you assumed the seller's mortgage, the seller must also be listed on your creditor list. Was your mortgage guaranteed by the VA, FHA, or FMHA? If so, they need to be listed, too. Did you ever sell a house? If you did, was the mortgage paid off or did the buyer assume your mortgage? If the mortgage was not paid off, it must be listed in your case as well.

Chapter 7 and cars, motorcycles and other vehicles

You may be buying a car, motorcycle or truck and making monthly payments. If you want to keep the vehicle you must keep the payments current. Otherwise, the creditor can go to the court and get an order permitting repossession of the vehicle.

It's best to make payments in person at the lender's office or to mail the payments by certified mail seven days before they are due. If the creditor returns the payment to you, or refuses to accept your payment, speak to your attorney immediately.

If you were delinquent before you filed your bankruptcy, even by one day, you should phone in and get the number of your bankruptcy and the date of filing, and let the bank or finance company know about the bankruptcy. This will stop any pending repossession.

Changing your mind

Every once in a while we have a client who signs bankruptcy papers, then changes his or her mind about filing.

This is a little like going to Las Vegas, getting married, and then deciding you don't want to be married. It's a lot easier to get married than it is to get a divorce. It's also easier to file bankruptcy than it is to get out of it.

Once your case has been filed, it is noted on your credit record even if you change your mind. A Chapter 13 can usually be dismissed or withdrawn with little difficulty. It is much more difficult to withdraw a Chapter 7 case and it is time-consuming and expensive to do so.

If you should change your mind, remember that your attorney has still done the work and you will still owe the fee for filing the bankruptcy.

Life after bankruptcy

A lot of myths surround bankruptcy – people believe they won't be able to get credit for seven years or that they can't pay a creditor after a debt has been listed in a bankruptcy petition.

This is just not true!

You can buy a house, a car, furniture, and you can move after a bankruptcy. Life goes on. Of course, your rent or mortgage and utility bills will go on, too. After you file, you will have to pay these and any new debts you acquire, if you expect to keep the items you have purchased.

10

Exemptions: What You Keep In Chapter 7 And Chapter 13

One day, a woman came to my office for an initial consultation. After we had analyzed her financial situation and come to the conclusion that the best option for her was to file a Chapter 7 bankruptcy, she became concerned about what personal property she might lose.

As I began to tell her that most of her property would be exempt, she twisted her wedding ring on her finger.

"Well I've put on so much weight since I got married, that if they want my wedding ring, they'll have to cut my finger off," she said. The fact is, you can have an expensive wedding ring — worth say, $5,000 or more — and the courts cannot take it away. The wedding ring is what the law refers to as "exempt."

What is an exemption?

An exemption is a right given to individuals by federal and state law so that they may keep part of their property free from seizure by creditors or a bankruptcy trustee.

The exemption laws in New York State were enacted with the philosophy that no one benefits if a debtor and his dependents are left homeless and on the edge of financial disaster. By allowing a debtor to keep a portion of his or her property exempt and free from creditors' claims, exemption laws encourage self-support so that debtors will not become dependent upon public assistance, such as welfare or food stamps.

Exemptions reflect the government's policy to provide a debtor a chance to start over with the essentials necessary to begin a new life. For those clients who file bankruptcy, exemptions help them obtain a fresh start.

How will I know what is exempt?

There is a common misconception that those who file Chapter 7 or Chapter 13 lose most or a substantial portion of what they own. This is generally not true. If the correct exemptions are claimed by debtors who file Chapter 7 or Chapter 13, they are allowed to keep a significant amount of the things they own.

When debtors consult with an attorney regarding bankruptcy, the attorney will need to know what assets they own, their value, and whether any assets were pledged as collateral on a loan. The attorney will then be able to explain how the appropriate bankruptcy case might benefit the debtor and what can be protected. The amount and type of assets a debtor can protect by claiming them as exempt can often determine whether a debtor would file Chapter 7 or Chapter 13 at all.

Keeping your home

New York's Homestead Exemption law allows you to protect your home when filing Chapter 7 or Chapter 13. The homestead exemption may be claimed on your house, condominium, cooperative apartment, mobile home, and the land on which the mobile home sits. The exemption may only be claimed on your principal place of residence.

The homestead exemption is not without limitations. It provides protection for your home only up to $10,000 in equity if you are the sole owner, or up to $20,000 in equity for married co-owners. The simple definition of equity is the amount you would be left with if you sold your home and paid off all the mortgages and any outstanding property taxes.

For example, if a married couple owns a $50,000 house with a $30,000 mortgage, the $20,000 equity in the property is exempt — neither creditors nor the bankruptcy trustee can touch it.

The homestead exemption does not protect you from the non-payment of real estate taxes; if you owe taxes on the home, you must pay them. Even an exempt homestead may be sold for non-payment of taxes.

Also, the exemption does not apply to mortgage foreclosures, and will not protect a person sued in an action for foreclosure of a mortgage on a residence. Although filing a Chapter 7 or Chapter 13 may stop a mortgage foreclosure from proceeding, the homestead exemption only protects that portion of your home equity allowed by law. The homestead exemption, however, does protect you against most other debts and obligations.

One Very Important Fact About The Homestead Exemption

Many clients are confused as to how the home exemption laws work. If they own a home, and pledged the home as collateral on a loan, they must keep paying that loan or they will lose the home. You do not get out of a home mortgage, home equity loan or a collateral mortgage by filing bankruptcy. You may only claim as exempt a portion of the value of the home that exceeds the mortgage.

An overview of the assets that are exempt in New York State:

Homestead

Real property, a home or an interest in a cooperative apartment, mobile home or condominium (up to a value of $10,000 of equity for an individual or $20,000 for a couple if the home is jointly owned).

Wages

Earned but unpaid wages — 90 percent of earned but unpaid wages received within 60 days of filing bankruptcy.

Tools of Trade

Necessary working tools, including mechanic's tools, farm machinery, professional instruments to a value of $600.

Personal Property

- Wearing apparel
- Equity in a motor vehicle up to $2,400 per debtor
- $2,500 in cash, bank deposits, U.S. savings bonds or tax refunds, if the individual does not own a home
- Most furniture and appliances
- Wedding ring
- A watch to a value of $35
- Domestic animals to a value of $450
- Security deposits to a landlord and utility companies
- Personal injury recoveries to a value of $7,500 and loss of future earnings
- Wrongful death recoveries

A debtor is limited to an aggregate value of $5,000 for all personal property exemptions. The debtor may exempt $2,500 in cash if the homestead exemption is not claimed, and if it does not put the debtor above the $5,000 exemptions limit.

Insurance

- Life insurance policies
- Disability insurance benefits – periodic payments up to $400 per month
- Annuities, if reasonable and necessary for the support of the debtor and family
- Insurance claims for damage to exempt property

Pensions and IRA Accounts

One hundred percent of pensions and IRA accounts, up to the amount necessary to support the debtor and his or her dependents

Public Benefits

- Social Security benefits
- Unemployment compensation
- Public assistance
- Veterans benefits
- Crime victim reparations
- Workers' Compensation

Alimony, Support and Maintenance

- Exempt to the extent necessary for support

What about assets that are not exempt?

You may have some property in a rare case that is not protected by the exemption laws. The following may happen to that property:

1. You could buy the property back from the Chapter 7 trustee over a short period of time. You would pay the liquidation value of the item.

2. Any items with a nominal value may not be of interest to the trustee, and he or she may allow you to keep them without paying anything for them. For example, if you have already claimed your primary automobile as exempt and you have a second car with a value of $700, the trustee will probably allow you to keep that vehicle and not require you to pay any money at all to the bankruptcy estate.

3. You might choose to file a Chapter 13 plan instead of a Chapter 7. In this way, you would pay the fair market value of the non-exempt items in small payments over three to five years. For example, if you own $5,000 in non-exempt assets, and want to keep those assets, you could make payments to your unsecured creditors through the Chapter 13 plan over a period of up to five years to cover the value of the assets. In a Chapter 13 plan, you have to offer your unsecured creditors as much as they would receive in a Chapter 7 liquidation.

4. If you aren't interested in keeping the non-exempt items, you can surrender them to the Chapter 7 trustee, pay nothing to the Chapter 7 trustee, and obtain a fresh start free from debt.

Well, why don't I just sell my non-exempt assets and buy exempt assets?

The issue of whether a debtor is allowed to protect property from creditors by selling it and converting it to types of property that are exempt, has been troubling for the courts. In most instances, the question arises when a Chapter 7 or Chapter 13 debtor has converted non-exempt assets to exempt assets during the year before bankruptcy.

The Bankruptcy Code provides that the court could deny the debtor a discharge if, within one year before bankruptcy, the debtor made a transfer with the intent to hinder, delay or defraud creditors.

> *It is important to have a clear understanding of how exemption laws work before your case is filed. Your attorney will ask many questions about what you own in order to determine what property is protected. If your case is handled properly, there should be no surprises about what you can keep and what you might lose by filing bankruptcy.*

Summary

In most instances, the equity in the debtor's home, the equity in the automobile, as well as the furniture, clothing, and other items of importance are protected when a debtor files a Chapter 7 or Chapter 13. It is the rare bankruptcy case that requires a debtor to lose property.

11

When Money Problems Threaten The Small Business Owner

The evidence that small businesses contributed greatly to the growth in the economy and employment in the past decade is undisputed. What is also undisputed is the fact that a substantial number of all businesses that have opened within the previous five years folded and filed either Chapter 7, 11, or 13.

The entrepreneurs I see in my office every day are suffering from two sources of stress — stress from business problems, and the same stresses felt by consumers in financial trouble.

Experts at the Buffalo office of the Small Business Administration estimate that 85 percent to 90 percent of all entrepreneurs must put up personal property as collateral to finance their businesses.

For example, the restaurateur whose business goes belly up will have a

large bill at the restaurant supply house and a loan at the bank for working capital, along with his charge accounts at the local store, an automobile loan and medical expenses. The bank loan may be secured by the bank having filed a mortgage on his or her home.

Even if our restaurateur gives up on his business and takes a well paying salaried position, his debts may far outpace his income.

What do you do if your business has financial problems?

In some instances, it is possible for a business to work out arrangements with creditors without the need for filing a bankruptcy case. Lenders may be willing to restructure the debt repayment if they believe the financial circumstances of the business are only temporary.

Secured creditors may also be willing to stretch out payments. Secured creditors may propose to work out an alternative payment plan with you rather than repossessing their collateral from which they may never recover the full amount of the loan. It is imperative for the business to pay its payroll taxes; these are non-dischargeable debts in bankruptcy, and will be a personal liability of the owners.

If a business' difficulties cannot be resolved, bankruptcy may be the way to go. There are three types of bankruptcy proceedings available to businesses. The first is a liquidation under Chapter 7 of the Code. The second in the case of nonincorporated proprietorships is Chapter 13 (the general principles of Chapter 7 and Chapter 13 also apply in business cases). And the third is a proceeding under Chapter 11.

The point in time at which the bankruptcy case is filed is extremely relevant because the filing of the bankruptcy obtains the automatic stay for the business. Once the automatic stay takes effect no further legal action can be brought against the company. A primary reason for filing a bankruptcy petition is the ability to obtain the automatic stay.

A typical Chapter 7 business bankruptcy

In a typical Chapter 7 business bankruptcy, the majority of the debt owed by the client's business will be discharged if the client is doing business as a DBA.

If the business is a corporation, the corporate debts don't get discharged but the creditors stop taking action once the case is filed. If there are corporate assets — with value and there is no lien against those assets — the trustee will liquidate them and distribute the proceeds among the creditors.

Once the Chapter 7 bankruptcy is filed, a trustee is appointed. It is the trustee's job to review the schedules and question the debtor about his or her affairs. If there are assets in the business that are unsecured and can be sold, the trustee will sell the business assets and distribute the proceeds to the company's creditors. In many Chapter 7 bankruptcies, unsecured creditors receive little if any dividend. The business assets may be of little value or are fully secured and are taken by secured creditors.

A business Chapter 13 case

In a business Chapter 13, the primary purpose of the reorganization is to keep the business going. What the creditors receive will depend upon the cash flow of the business, the value of the business assets, and the type of debt the company has. To qualify for Chapter 13, the business must not be incorporated, and must have under $1 million in debt.

For example, let's suppose that following the filing of a Chapter 13 plan, the company expects to have profits after all expenses of $2,000 per month. Let's further assume the business owner needs $1,500 per month to pay his personal living expenses. Therefore, there is $500 left. Further assume that the business owner has $3,000 in nondischargeable taxes, $100,000 of unsecured debt and nominal assets. A Chapter 13 plan might be proposed whereby $450 per month would be paid to the Chapter 13 trustee for a period of 60 months, and the plan would pay the nondischargeable taxes in full, and a small percentage on the dollar to the unsecured creditors. The balance of all the debt would be forgiven. The business continues to be owned and operated by the debtor. And, the debtor loses no assets.

A Chapter 13 reorganization begins when a debtor files a petition, schedule of assets and liabilities, Statement of Financial Affairs, and a Chapter 13 plan.

The Chapter 13 plan must meet certain requirements

In order to process the bankruptcy, the debtor will need the following information: a creditor list, income information, a list of property, and a detailed list of income and expenses. The debtor will also have to disclose all inventory, work in process, etc.

On a periodic basis as set by the Chapter 13 trustee, the debtor is required to file a report of income and expenses, including all taxes paid, and identification of all insurance coverage. Failure to file these reports as requested by the Chapter 13 trustee can result in the case being dismissed or converted to Chapter 7.

The debtor is required to appear at the 341 Meeting (meeting of creditors). A $160 filing fee is also required when the Chapter 13 petition is filed. When the case is filed, most actions by creditors will stop. As with Chapter 7 and Chapter 11, the law prohibits creditors from initiating any lawsuit, wage garnishments, or calls demanding payment. All creditors listed in the bankruptcy petition will receive notice of the filing.

The Chapter 13 plan must meet certain requirements that are set out in the Bankruptcy Code. Creditors are classified according to the nature of their debt. The court must also determine that the plan is feasible, has been filed in good faith, and that the unsecured creditors in the Chapter 13 plan will receive as much as they would have received if a Chapter 7 had been filed. Payments under the Chapter 13 plan must begin within 30 days of the filing. If the plan is confirmed by the court, all creditors are bound by its terms.

Approximately 36 to 60 months following the confirmation of the plan, the debtor will receive a discharge.

What are the most important aspects of the Chapter 13 business case?

First of all, priority debts, such as most taxes, must be paid in full by the debtor, through the Chapter 13 plan.

Second, the unsecured creditors will usually receive a much smaller percentage of what they are actually owed. In many instances, the unsecured creditors in a Chapter 13 case will only receive what they would have obtained if a Chapter 7 straight bankruptcy had been filed, and in the vast majority of cases, the percentage paid is small.

If there are secured creditors, such as a creditor who has a lien against business equipment, those secured creditors are generally "crammed down." This means the secured creditors will receive only the liquidation value of their collateral in the Chapter 13 plan, rather than what is due. For example, if a secured creditor such as a bank is owed $30,000 on business equipment, but the appraised liquidation value of the equipment is only $6,000, in many instances that creditor will only receive the $6,000 with a small amount of interest at the rate of $100 per month for 60 months.

The main advantage of Chapter 13 over Chapter 7 is that the debtor is allowed to continue to operate the business, and keep all of the business assets.

Filing for Chapter 11

If the small business has incorporated, the owner cannot turn to Chapter 13 for relief. He or she can still use a Chapter 7 liquidation, or if there is interest in keeping the business going, a Chapter 11 or "business reorganization" can be filed. Although Chapter 11 is typically a reorganizational move, most courts agree that it can also be used to liquidate the business if necessary. Individuals may also file Chapter 11; however, an individual will probably discover the requirements of Chapter 11 are extremely difficult and costly.

In a Chapter 11, the debtor is referred to as "debtor in possession" and can continue operation of the business. When a case is filed, the U.S. trustee will appoint a committee of creditors holding unsecured claims.

A Chapter 11 begins when a debtor files a petition, schedule of assets and liabilities, and a Statement of Financial Affairs.

In order to complete the initial filing, the debtor will need the following information: creditor list, income information, a list of property and a detailed list of income and expenses. The debtor will also have to disclose all inventory, work in process, etc.

Each and every month, the debtor is required to file a report of income and expenses, including all taxes paid, and an identification of all insurance coverage. Failure to file these reports can result in the case being dismissed or converted to Chapter 7.

A disclosure statement must set forth all the information the creditor would need or want to know

Until a plan of reorganization is confirmed, the debtor must pay a quarterly fee to the office of the U.S. Trustee. The U.S. Trustee is a division of the Department of Justice and is the "watchdog" of the bankruptcy system.

The debtor is required to appear at the 341 Meeting (meeting of creditors). An $800 filing fee is also required when the Chapter 11 petition is filed. When the case is filed, most actions by creditors will stop. As with Chapter 7 and Chapter 13, the law prohibits creditors from initiating any lawsuits, wage garnishments or calls demanding payment. All creditors listed in the bankruptcy petition will receive notice of the filing.

During the first 120 days of the Chapter 11, only the debtor is permitted to file a disclosure statement and plan of reorganization. The debtor may also obtain an extension of this exclusive period for cause if requested before the 120 days expires. Following the exclusive period, any creditor may file a plan of reorganization and disclosure statement.

A disclosure statement must set forth all the information the creditor would need or want to know in order to decide whether or not to approve the debtor's reorganization plan. Financial information should also contain facts and data to support projections and other representations.

The plan must meet certain requirements. Creditors are classified according to the nature of their debt. The court must also determine that the plan will not result in the need for further reorganization and the debtor is able to meet the terms.

Not all classes must vote on a plan, but at least two-thirds of the total dollar amount and more than one-half of allowed claims casting ballots in a voting class must accept the plan in order to obtain court approval. On some occasions, the court may confirm a plan even if this formula is not met.

A confirmed plan is a new contract between the debtor and the creditors.

Upon confirmation of the plan, the debtor is discharged from the pre-petition obligations because those obligations have been replaced by the new ones proposed under the plan.

Upon the substantial completion of the plan, the debtor files a request for final decree. Once the plan has been consummated, a final decree is entered.

A fresh start for businesses, too

A business with debt problems deserves a second chance. In times of poor economic growth, the risks for start-up businesses increase. Yet, we need those businesses to stimulate the sluggish economy and generate more employment.

If we are to foster the entrepreneurial spirit in this country, we must also preserve the option of bankruptcy or reorganization in order to provide those who fail with the option to start over.

12

Foreclosure: What To Do If It Looms?

If you are having problems with your mortgage, you must read this chapter. It provides tips that may save your home from foreclosure. This chapter will also provide a basic understanding of what happens when a foreclosure takes place.

It's the American dream, the rite of passage that means you are established — it's home ownership.

Owning your home takes on social significance that is second only to your occupation. Your home is probably the largest asset you have, and it is one that usually appreciates in value, unlike your car or furniture.

Stay current with mortgage payments

Mortgage payments should be your first priority. Do not pay other low priority debts such as credit cards, store charges, or medical bills ahead of the mortgage. If you fail to pay low priority debts for several months, there may be few negative ramifications. However, if you skip two or three mortgage payments, you may lose your house.

Foreclosure generally takes place because the mortgage is not being paid in a timely manner. When a homeowner is behind on mortgage payments, the loan is said to be delinquent.

Since your home is intertwined with friends, neighbors, schools, status and work, its loss through foreclosure is a very emotional experience.

As financial traumas go, the only correspondence that horrifies consumers more than an impending garnishment of wages or seizure of a bank account, is a summons and complaint that the homeowner is about to lose the family home.

How the foreclosure process works

The bank or lender files a lawsuit naming the borrower as a defendant. In the lawsuit the bank sets out the debt and the mortgage and indicates it is in default. The lender will then request that the court grant the following relief against the homeowner (defendant):

1. That the defendant's rights in the property be terminated.
2. That the real estate be sold at public auction.
3. That the money owed to the bank be paid from the sale proceeds.

"To the above named defendants," the Summons began in large black letters, *"you are hereby summoned to answer the complaint in this action. . . . In case of your failure to appear or answer, judgment will be taken against you by default. . . . This is an action to foreclose a mortgage on premises situate in the County of Monroe."*

The lawsuit papers consist of a summons and complaint and are delivered to the homeowner. These lawsuit papers give you formal notification about the case being brought against you.

The foreclosure papers and Notice of Pendency are filed at the county clerk's office where the property is located. The filing of these lawsuit papers at the county clerk's office informs the public that a lawsuit affecting title to your property has been started.

Unless the property owner successfully contests the foreclosure, a judgment is entered for the lender. Approximately six months to a year after the lawsuit has been started, the real estate is sold under court supervision. A foreclosure of real estate is a poorly advertised auction. In most instances, no one except the lender even attends the auction, and generally the lender will be the only bidder at the auction, and will bid no more than the balance of the debt.

What should homeowners do when they fall behind on mortgage payments?

Consult with an attorney.

Many people fall behind on their mortgage payments because of divorce, illness, job loss, etc. The first thing you must do if you are having a problem

making your mortgage payments, is get serious. There are many people who put their head in the sand and delay doing anything until it is too late. Four or five delinquent payments can lead to a foreclosure summons. Some lenders may even begin the foreclosure process after 90 days.

Because foreclosure will terminate your interest in the real estate, get help immediately. In many cases, homeowners delay consulting with an attorney until it is too late, or walk away from the situation.

Negotiate with the mortgage holder

Many lenders are interested in working out some alternatives. The sooner the borrower makes the lender aware of the problem, the more likely the lender is able to assist the borrower. One of the most important strategies is for the homeowner to work out with the lender a temporary delay in payments or a period of reduced payments.

If your home is insured through a government agency such as the VA or FHA, check into assistance programs offered by those agencies to prevent foreclosures. Conventional loans insured by private mortgage insurance companies may also provide a source of assistance.

List the house for sale

If you can no longer afford to make your mortgage payments, the homeowner may decide to list the home for sale. If you find a buyer and sell your home privately before the foreclosure sale takes place, you will be able to get your equity out of the home.

Whether you file Chapter 7 or Chapter 13, you will be able to keep your home

Filing bankruptcy can stop a foreclosure

Whether you file Chapter 7 or Chapter 13, you will be able to keep your home but only if you continue to make your regular monthly mortgage payments. If Chapter 7 is filed, you must make suitable arrangements to catch up the delinquent mortgage payments.

If you select Chapter 13, you may be able to include the mortgage arrearages in the Chapter 13 payment plan and pay those off over three to five years. If you do file Chapter 13, it is important to remember that all future post-petition mortgage payments must be made by you directly and on time.

For example, a Chapter 13 plan may allow a homeowner owing $6,000 in past due mortgage payments to pay $100 a month plus a small amount of interest over a period of five years to catch up. During this time, the client must also pay the current mortgage payments on time.

As long as the payments through the 13 plan and post-petition mortgage payments are kept up, the bank cannot foreclose. The homeowner emerges from the Chapter 13 plan with the home, and his or her living situation intact.

The automatic stay

The filing of a petition in bankruptcy, whether it is a Chapter 7 or a Chapter 13, will stop most creditor actions against the debtor, including the foreclosure process. The creditor is not allowed to proceed with the foreclosure without first obtaining the court's permission. If you file a feasible Chapter 13 plan, and you are able to meet the other requirements of the Bankruptcy Code, the bankruptcy judge will, in most instances, not give the creditor permission to proceed.

Catching up your delinquent payments through Chapter 13

In most cases, individuals who have been delinquent with their mortgage payments use Chapter 13 if they want to keep their home. Chapter 13 can stop the foreclosure sale of the home and allow the homeowner three to five years to catch up on the delinquent payments, as long as the current payments are made.

To qualify for Chapter 13, the homeowner must have a steady source of income, which could be from a paycheck, unemployment insurance, or Social Security Disability, among other things. Secured debt can total no more than $750,000, and unsecured debt no more than $250,000.

The Chapter 13 plan may propose that the property be sold

In some instances, your home may become too much of a burden in terms of upkeep and continuing the mortgage payments. The Chapter 13 plan would propose that the homeowner would make current mortgage payments, but the house would be sold within 12 to 18 months from the time the Chapter 13 plan is filed.

This would allow the homeowner to obtain the equity in the home and pay off the mortgage.

How Chapter 7 might help

The homeowner may consider filing Chapter 7 and turning the house over to the mortgage company. Or, if the homeowner has struggled to stay current with the mortgage but cannot pay other bills, Chapter 7 bankruptcy can discharge those other debts, making it a bit easier to pay the mortgage.

An additional option

If there is little or no equity in your property (for example, if your home is worth $50,000 and your mortgage is worth $45,000) and you can't afford the property any longer, consider staying in the house until the foreclosure is complete. Since the foreclosure process can take six to 12 months to complete, some clients stay in the house and don't make any mortgage payments. During this time they can save money to rent an apartment.

Conclusion

In some cases, the homeowner may still be able to stop foreclosure by making up the missed payments. Before foreclosure becomes a reality, check into as many options as possible to protect your home.

Pay Your Mortgage First

The creditors that make the most noise by calling and threatening are often not the most important to pay. Often low priority type creditors can do little other than make a lot of noise. Mortgage, rent, utility and car creditors are the ones to be paid first if you can.

13

Protecting The Family Car

The repossession process

The car creditor has the right to take your car even if you are only a few weeks late in making your payments. Under New York State law, the car creditor does not need to obtain permission from the court before they repossess the car. The creditor may on its own just come during the middle of the night and take the car right out of your driveway. In most instances, the creditor will not even notify you in advance that the repossession is going to take place.

What should you do to prevent your car from being repossessed?

If you are having temporary difficulties, you may decide not to pay credit card debts, doctor bills, or other low priority debts ahead of the car payments. Not paying low priority debts for several months will have little or no consequences. However, if you skip a couple car payments, I can assure you that the car will be repossessed by the creditor who has a lien against the vehicle, such as General Motors Acceptance Company, Ford Motor Credit Company, ACSI, etc.

Some creditors may be willing to negotiate an arrangement where your monthly payments are lowered, or where one or two missed payments are put at the end of the loan. In situations where the loan is much higher than the value of the car, a workout will be a better deal for the creditor.

What about the personal property inside the car?

If you believe the vehicle may be repossessed, it is important to remove your personal possessions from the car. In many situations, property left inside the car somehow disappears following a repossession. If items are missing following a repossession, you can attempt to require the creditor to pay for the items not returned, but you probably will fail.

What can bankruptcy do?

You may consider filing a Chapter 13 or Chapter 7 bankruptcy if you believe your car is in jeopardy. Upon filing the bankruptcy case, the automatic stay takes effect. Once the automatic stay is in effect, no one is permitted to take your car. In some instances, the car creditor will ask the bankruptcy court for permission to take the car. If you file a Chapter 13 plan, you generally provide to pay the car creditor the liquidation value of the car in the plan over 36 to 60 months, not what you owe. For example, if you owe the car creditor $10,000 but the car is worth only $4,000, you would pay the $4,000 back at $100 per month, plus a small amount of interest over a period of 36 to 60 months. The balance of the debt is referred to as the unsecured portion, and that is often forgiven in the Chapter 13 case.

If you file Chapter 7 and want to keep the vehicle, you must stay current with your payments, and you must agree to reaffirm and pay the car creditor every month according to the terms of the contract. If you fail to pay your regular monthly car payments following the filing of the Chapter 7 case, the car creditor will eventually obtain permission from the court to repossess the vehicle.

What happens if your car is repossessed?

If your car is repossessed, and you do not choose to file Chapter 7 or Chapter 13, you still have a right to reinstate your contract. Reinstating your contract allows you to recover the repossessed car, and pay only the back due payments and not the full amount of the loan. Remember, that reinstatement applies to loans and does not apply to car leases.

> Consider filing a Chapter 13 or Chapter 7 bankruptcy if you believe your car is in jeopardy

14

The Personal Side Of Bankruptcy

When Susan Jones came into my office, she was very depressed about the fact she was unable to pay the $100,000 she owed in credit card debt. Susan told me she had a $100,000 life insurance policy, and that she had actually thought about committing suicide so that the debts could be paid from the insurance benefits.

There's an old saying that suicide is a permanent solution to a temporary problem. Financial troubles and bankruptcy are temporary problems. They are painful at the moment, but in time you can get your life back on track.

Clients first come into my office under a great deal of stress. It's evident in their appearance. Their faces are often worn from the depression and anxiety they've been feeling. The circles under their eyes show their lack of sleep. During my initial conversation with these people, they sometimes find it difficult to concentrate or they become teary-eyed as they try to talk about their problem.

It's natural to feel some depression when experiencing financial problems. You have, in a sense, suffered a loss — the loss of your financial stability. This can make you feel angry and resentful, and you may find yourself turning these feelings inward. You may feel embarrassed or ashamed that you got into this kind of trouble. You might even feel guilty about it, especially if you think you brought it on yourself or could have prevented it from happening. Perhaps the problem was a long time in coming, but you didn't heed the warning signs. So now you feel like a failure. Or maybe you did recognize the problem, but you still feel like you failed.

Whatever the circumstances, you are probably feeling overwhelmed by the situation. Fears and confusion have taken over your daily life. Your financial troubles are all you can think about. What would your family and friends say if they knew you might file bankruptcy? Will you ever get credit again? Is your life ruined now? Will you ever feel normal again?

How bankruptcy might help

During an initial consultation, the first thing I do is assess your financial situation and help you decide whether bankruptcy is the right solution for your problem. If it is the right answer for you, bankruptcy will free you of your financial worries and get the creditors off your back. You'll get your life back to normal again.

If you file a Chapter 7 bankruptcy, most or all of your debts will be discharged and you won't have to pay them back. Your slate is wiped clean. You can start once again to build a better financial future.

If you file Chapter 13, you can satisfy any moral or ethical obligation you may feel to repay your debts, but you can do it by paying back only a portion of the debt. A plan is designed allowing you to make payments you can afford, which will be put toward the debts included in the plan. Payments are usually made over a period of three to five years.

In either case, once the bankruptcy petition is filed, your creditors can take no further action against you. The harassment ceases.

What will people think?

No one has to know you are filing bankruptcy, other than those directly involved with it. Your family and friends need not be told unless you choose to tell them. Only you can judge which people will help if they know and which ones will only hurt you, however well-intentioned their concerns.

> No one has to know you are filing bankruptcy

The stigma that was once attached to bankruptcy has lessened dramatically. But it still exists in the minds of some.

The fact is, there are still some people out there who have archaic views of bankruptcy. And why not? We are all raised to believe that bad things don't happen to good people. We're taught that if we work hard and follow the rules, we'll get the good things in life — a home, a car, savings and sufficient income to afford nice things for ourselves and our families. Honest, hard-working people don't go bankrupt.

In reality, these doctrines simply do not hold true.

Bankruptcies continue to climb

In the 1970's, under the Bankruptcy Act, approximately two million bankruptcies were filed througout the entire decade. In the 1980's, under the more liberal Bankruptcy Code, that number more than doubled to approximately five million. Currently, almost a million are filed every year.

All kinds of people file bankruptcy: rich and poor; famous people and those who are little-known; some who are highly ethical, and some who have little respect for ethics or the law. The reasons for their financial problems vary. Some have lost their jobs. Others have severe health problems and their medical expenses are more than they can handle. For still others, years of poor money management have finally taken their toll.

The bankruptcy laws were enacted to give us all the opportunity for a fresh start. Many individuals and corporations that are contributing to our economy today once filed a bankruptcy.

How will this affect my personal life?

The effect of bankruptcy on your life depends a lot on how constructively you handle it. The most significant events in our lives are said to be marriages, divorces, births, traumatic injury or illness, and deaths. Although bankruptcy can feel like a major event at the time, your outlook can help put it in perspective.

It's important not to spend a lot of time laying blame for your financial problems, either on yourself or on others. This is a futile waste of energy, and can take a toll on your family life, your friendships and your inner security. You'll feel that you have no control over your life and you'll lose confidence just when you need it most - when it's time to rebuild your life. No one is perfect. We all make mistakes, and your bankruptcy is an opportunity for you to get a fresh start while learning a better way to manage your finances.

... watch out for signs of depression

As I stated earlier, it's natural to feel some depression when you're having financial problems. Making the decision to file bankruptcy can intensify those feelings.

What can happen, however, is that you become so consumed by your financial situation that you don't realize you are suffering from depression.

If you are having financial difficulty and especially if you are going through bankruptcy, keep an eye out for these signals:

- You find little interest or pleasure in doing things you used to enjoy
- You feel down, depressed or angry
- You feel hopeless, worthless
- You feel a sense of doom — the worst possible thing that could ever happen is certain to happen to you
- You feel responsible for all the bad things that happen to you, while all the good things are due to luck
- You have trouble sleeping
- You have difficulty concentrating
- You're fidgety, nervous
- You feel a lack of energy
- You have multiple physical symptoms with no medical explanation
- You feel bad about yourself
- You have a poor appetite, or you overeat
- You abuse alcohol or other drugs
- You have suicidal thoughts

... talk to your doctor

Many people are afraid or unwilling to bring up the subject of depression with their physicians. They may feel their doctors are not interested in their emotional problems, or they may still feel the stigma often attached to emotional distress. Those kinds of problems can be frightening.

But depression and other emotional difficulties, like any medical problems, are best treated early, and will usually only get worse if left untreated.

If you think you may be experiencing depression, your best chance for getting help is to talk to your doctor about it, and the sooner the better.

... help is available

There is help available to anyone facing these struggles. For those who have medical coverage, their individual insurance policy or HMO contract will determine what services are covered and who can provide them. Those on Medicaid can seek the services of any physician or mental health practitioner who accepts Medicaid patients.

For those with no medical coverage, there are many organizations that provide financial aid, emotional support, medical assistance, counseling and other services to anyone going through difficult times. Fees vary depending on the type of service provided and the financial status of the person seeking help. Many services are offered totally free of charge.

Whatever a person's financial situation, there are many groups available to provide all kinds of support. A "help list" is located at the end of this chapter.

... do what you can to help yourself

Whether you are experiencing depression or just trying to stay as emotionally healthy as possible, there are things you can do to help yourself adjust to your new situation.

Talk about your problems. If you have a friend or relative who will lend a sympathetic ear, take advantage of it. If there are a few such people you can rely on, it will lessen the tendency to "unload" on one person. Keep in mind that they are only human, too. You can talk to them without overburdening them with your problems.

Find a support group. There are such groups for nearly every kind of problem, as well as for general emotional support while going through life changes.

Participate in community or church activities. Do some volunteer work. It's a great way to feel useful while getting your mind off your own troubles.

With your doctor's approval, get as much physical exercise as possible.

... it will get better

Over time, your bankruptcy will probably become less and less significant, until it's just an event that put you on a new road to financial health.

What about re-establishing credit?

Most credit applications will require you to disclose prior bankruptcies. It is still possible, however, to re-establish your credit over time (see Chapter 17, "How To Re-establish Credit"). The important question to ask yourself is whether you really want to go that route again. You will probably have to use credit for some purchases, but try using the pay-as-you-go approach as much as possible.

> Over time, your bankruptcy will probably become less and less significant

People who thought they could never live without credit cards have discovered a whole new way of life — paying cash. Some use the lay-away method whenever they can. Paying off the cost of the item <u>before</u> picking it up gives them a great feeling of control. And they feel like they're being "rewarded" when they receive their merchandise. Others have a savings account, and use it to save up for purchases, letting their money earn interest while accumulating enough for the purchase. Credit cards? They now consider them a burden.

A new beginning

Among all the emotions my clients experience when filing bankruptcy, they usually feel a sense of relief when they realize it is the "beginning of the end" of their financial problems. The knowledge that they will once again be on solid financial ground immediately raises their self-esteem. They are regaining control of their lives, step by step.

In the end, my clients see that filing bankruptcy was the first step toward a better financial future.

A listing of community groups that can help you through the difficult period begins on the next page.

Help List

Organizations
that can
assist you

The following information was derived primarily from the Human Services Directory, a guide produced by the Reynolds Information Center, and the United Way program directory. For additional information about these and many other community, government and social agencies, please call the Reynolds Information Center at 428-7372.

Counseling Services — Emergency

Health Assoc. of Rochester — Life Line / 423-9490
24 hours a day / 7 days a week

Provides 24-hour free and confidential telephone counseling services; crisis intervention for medical and mental health problems; human services information and referral

Area served: Monroe and nearby counties

Counseling Services — General

Action for a Better Community, Inc. / 325-5116

Operates a variety of programs designed to build self-sufficiency in low-income families and individuals; offers budget counseling services and a weatherization program

Area served: Monroe and nearby counties

Catholic Family Center / 546-7220

Provides individual and family counseling, emergency financial services

Area served: Monroe and nearby counties

Family Services of Rochester, Inc. / 232-1840

Provides individual and family counseling; mental health clinic; outpatient alcohol and drug clinic

Area served: Monroe and nearby counties

Jewish Family Services of Rochester, Inc. / 461-0110

Provides individual and family counseling; group therapy; various other services

Area served: Monroe and nearby counties

Mental Health Association / 716-325-3145

Referral to mental health services, self-help groups and private therapists

Area served: Monroe and nearby counties

The Housing Council / 546-3700

Provides counseling to persons with housing-related problems

Area served: Monroe and nearby counties

United Way of Greater Rochester, Inc. / 454-2770

Provides assistance for a variety of problems and needs

Area served: Monroe and nearby counties

Financial Assistance

Catholic Family Center / 546-7220

Provides individual and family counseling, emergency financial services

Area served: Monroe and nearby counties

Monroe County Department of Social Services / 274-6000

Offers general information and referral to appropriate division; help available includes financial assistance, Medicaid, food stamps and help with heating bills, all subject to eligibility

Area served: Monroe County

Salvation Army / 987-9500

Provides emergency shelter; special assistance to families, elderly, youths and substance abusers

Area served: Monroe County

United Way of Greater Rochester, Inc. / 454-2770

Offers assistance for a variety of problems and needs

Area served: Monroe and nearby counties

Medical Assistance

Medical Society of the County of Monroe, Inc. / 473-7573

Provides physician referral service; mediation of physician-patient problems; publications

Area served: Monroe and nearby counties

United Way of Greater Rochester, Inc. / 454-2770

Provides assistance for a variety of problems and needs

Area served: Monroe and nearby counties

15

Student Loans And Bankruptcy

Because of the increasing costs of education, students sometimes leave school owing student loan creditors thousands of dollars which are payable for years, at the rate of hundreds of dollars per month. We have seen these same creditors, schools and guaranty agencies taking strict measures to collect these debts.

A client who obtains either a Chapter 13 or a Chapter 7 discharge can obtain a discharge of the student loan or tuition if one of the following tests is met, (1) the student loan or tuition is over seven years old or (2) repayment would prove to be an "undue hardship."

The seven year rule

The Bankruptcy Code makes student loans dischargeable in bankruptcy if the debt is more than seven years old.

How you count the seven years is important. You begin counting seven years from the date the debt became due. You also have the right to a grace period before your repayment period begins. (Your parents do not receive a grace period for a plus loan.) Your grace period begins when you leave school or drop below half-time status. The length of your grace period is shown on your promissory note.

For example, if you graduated from a university on May 31, the student loan or tuition might become due six months from that date. But you have to carefully review the student loan papers you signed to ascertain the length of the grace period following the graduation or following the time you dropped out of school.

In addition, if you requested and were granted a deferment, the time the student loan was deferred is added on to the seven years. For example, if you requested and were granted a deferment for a period of one year, the loan has to be more than eight years old in order to discharge it in bankruptcy.

Keep Copies Of All Correspondence

When communicating with your student loan creditors always keep a copy of all letters you send them. In addition, always get the names of the persons you speak with as well as their telephone numbers. Write down what they tell you.

Is the debt more than seven years old?

If there is any question as to the age of the loan, it is important to clarify this issue. If you have a question, send a registered letter under the Freedom of Information Act to the guaranty agency, the lender and any collection agency involved, or the school if it is a bill for tuition. In New York State the New York State Higher Education Services Corp. is the guarantor of most student loans. You would request:

1. the date the debt became due, and

2. the length and number of any deferments that may have been granted.

You should send in a bank draft for $10 with each request to cover any possible costs, and be sure to keep a copy of the letter you send.

It may take several months for a response, or there may be no response at all. If these organizations fail to respond, you may wish to contact the office of your Congressman or U.S. Senator for help. You may obtain the addresses for your government representatives by looking in the telephone book under U.S. Government offices.

It is important to obtain the proper information. If you file your petition just one day too early, the student loan will not be discharged under the seven year rule. Here is a sample letter:

(Date)

New York State Higher Education
Services Corp.
99 Washington Ave.
Albany, NY 12255

RE: Student Loan Debt of Marshall Alloy
       SS#: 123-45-6789

To Whom It May Concern:

I am currently in the process of organizing all the correspondence I have received from New York State Higher Education Services Corp. However, I now realize I will need additional information on my loan that may be found in records maintained by your office.

Specifically, I am requesting the date my loan became due. I do not need to know the date of default, but rather I need to know the exact date the debt became due. A debt usually becomes due six or nine months following graduation or exiting school. I am also requesting the number and length of any deferments granted, if any, on this loan.

I have made numerous telephone calls to your agency regarding the aforementioned two questions, but to no avail. I am repeatedly told that the information is not accessible. Hence, in October of 1993, I wrote you a letter detailing my queries.

Therefore, I am once again requesting that the New York State Higher Education Services Corporation please release said pertinent documents necessary to ascertain the correct answers to the above questions. I make this inquiry under the Freedom of Information Act, as provided for under state and federal laws.

Thank you very much for your prompt attention and consideration in facilitating this matter. Enclosed please find a check for $10 to cover any costs incurred during your search under the Freedom of Information Act.

Sincerely,

Marshall Alloy

cc: (Your Senator or member of Congress)

Proving undue hardship is another way to discharge the student loan through bankruptcy

Bankruptcy courts across the country have struggled to give proper definition to the term "undue hardship." The Second Circuit Court of Appeals, which is the highest federal court in New York State, has established a three-part test to determine whether an individual qualifies for the discharge of student loans due to hardship. The test, commonly referred to as the Brunner test, requires:

1. that the debtor cannot maintain, based on current income and expenses, a "minimal" standard of living if forced to repay the loans;

2. that additional circumstances exist indicating that this state of affairs is likely to persist for a significant portion of the repayment period;

3. that the debtor has made good faith efforts to repay the loans.

Many people are able to meet the first and third part of the test. Unless all three parts are met, however, the court will not discharge the loan based on hardship.

> Bankruptcy courts have struggled to give proper definition to the term "undue hardship"

To meet the standards in Part 1:

A budget that will not balance will weigh in favor of the debtor. The debtor must prove that legitimate expenditures for necessities exceed income. The expenses must be reasonable and necessary, and the budget must show the debtor and dependents cannot maintain a minimal standard of living. Often, the budget will show that legitimate needs such as auto repairs and medical care have been postponed.

In addition, a look at the debtor's financial future is necessary. The court must determine whether it is less likely, likely only with extreme difficulty, or unlikely at all that the debtor will be able to honor the commitment to repay the loan in the foreseeable future.

To meet the standards in Part 2:

Most individuals cannot meet the standards required to meet Part 2 of the test. This section requires exceptional circumstances that suggest continuing inability to pay over an extended period of time. The following factors will be helpful to meet Part 2 of the test:

- the debtor or debtor's dependents are ill or disabled
- the debtor is elderly
- lack of usable job skills
- history of minimum wage jobs
- existence of a large number of dependents
- evidence of substantial effort to find work
- may require therapist to testify that ability to work is impaired
- may require testimony of an expert that there is total foreclosure of job prospects in area of training
- two or more years have elapsed since debtor last attended school
- no prospects of future improvement
- a combination of the above factors

To meet the standards in Part 3:

If the client has been guilty of bad faith in repaying the loan, or has extravagant spending habits, it is quite likely the court will rule against the discharge of debt. On the other hand, if a good faith effort has been made by the debtor, the court may decide that the loan can be discharged in bankruptcy. Actions such as attempts to make payments or negotiating an extension or a lower payment plan are examples of a good faith effort.

A careful analysis of your financial situation must be made by your bankruptcy attorney. If you meet all three tests, your student loan or tuition may be discharged in Chapter 7 or Chapter 13 based on hardship following a trial before the bankruptcy judge.

Dealing with student loans in Chapter 13 when the seven year rule and hardship do not apply

At the moment the Chapter 13 petition is filed with the court, the automatic stay takes effect. All creditors, including student loan creditors, must cease collection efforts against the debtor. The debtor can list the student loan creditor in the Chapter 13 plan and propose that the debt during the Chapter 13 be treated like any other unsecured debt.

You must remember that student loans in most cases will not be dischargeable. It is therefore in the individual's best interest to attempt to pay as much on the student loan through the Chapter 13 plan as possible. Your Chapter 13 plan might propose to pay student loan debt at 100% and other unsecured debt at 5%. For example, if you owe $20,000 on credit card debts, a Chapter 13 plan may propose to pay those creditors at the rate of five cents on the dollar, so they would receive a total of $1,000 through the Chapter 13 plan. The $5,000 owed on the student loans may be paid back at 100 percent through the Chapter 13 plan. This plan might cost $125.00 per month. When you file Chapter 13, you must pay into your plan as much as your budget will allow during a three-year period.

For the individual who pays 100 percent plus interest on the student loan during the course of the Chapter 13 plan, that is it. There are no collection activities following the case.

Most of our clients cannot afford to pay the student loan creditor 100 percent in the Chapter 13 plan. Most pay only 5 to 10 percent on the student loan while they are in the Chapter 13 plan. While they are in the plan, the student loan creditor cannot bother them. They get a breathing spell, a chance to improve their situation.

For the majority of clients who only pay a percentage on the dollar on the student loan during the plan, the student loan creditor can attempt to collect the balance following the discharge. If you have made payments in this manner, we suggest you contact the student loan creditor upon completion of the plan and arrange a satisfactory payment schedule for the balance.

Remember that while you are in the Chapter 13 plan, the interest on the loan continues to accumulate.

Chapter 7 and the non-dischargeable student loan/tuition

As mentioned previously, most student loans and tuition will not be discharged by filing Chapter 7. However, upon filing the petition with the bankruptcy court and for a period of about 90 days thereafter, the automatic stay is in effect.

During this period, the student loan creditors will not be allowed to engage in collection activities. Once the debtor receives a discharge from the bankruptcy court, the student loan creditors will contact the debtor and resume collection activity.

Therefore, it is very important to be prepared to deal with these creditors once you receive a discharge.

Conclusion

This is a complicated area of the law. Discuss all of the possible options with your attorney. In many cases, a favorable resolution can be found.

For More Information

The U.S. Dept. of Education produced a booklet outlining a variety of issues relating to student loans and tuition. To obtain a free copy of "The Student Guide" contact:

> *Federal Student Aid Information Center*
> *P.O. Box 84*
> *Washington, DC 20044-0084*

16

Discharging Taxes Through Bankruptcy

Can taxes be canceled in bankruptcy?

It depends.

Let's suppose you owe back taxes to the IRS or New York State and you don't have the money to pay them in full. In addition, you don't have the ability to pay on a monthly installment arrangement. Where can you turn for help? The answer may be the Bankruptcy Code.

Through bankruptcy, an individual may be able to discharge or cancel the legal obligation to pay a tax. The Bankruptcy Code contains specific provisions that establish whether a tax can be discharged in a bankruptcy proceeding.

Since 1977, when I began practicing law, I have met with many clients who have had delinquent taxes they owed to the IRS or New York State. Most clients are wage earning individuals who owe income taxes. Others operate a business — either as a DBA or a corporation — and owe payroll, sales tax, employment tax or Social Security payments.

There is a common misconception that taxes are never discharged in bankruptcy. This is not true. In a substantial number of cases, taxes can be discharged or eliminated in bankruptcy.

When clients owe personal income taxes, and the taxes are over three years old, in many cases the tax, interest and penalties may be discharged in Chapter 7 or 13.

Discharging taxes through Chapter 7

There are six basic tests that need to be met before a tax can be discharged in a Chapter 7 case. The taxes:

- must be personal income taxes
- must be over three years old
- have been assessed more than 240 days prior to the filing of the bankruptcy
- must be a tax for which a tax return was filed by the taxpayer at least two years prior to bankruptcy
- must not be associated with a fraudulent tax return or willful evasion of tax
- must no longer be assessable although never previously assessed

If these tests are met, and the IRS or New York State has not filed a lien against the taxpayer for the tax year in issue, the tax may be discharged in Chapter 7.

Example:

The IRS has levied your wages, and attached your bank account, claiming you owe $30,000 in back taxes, interest and penalties. You and your spouse have a combined income of $37,000. There is $5,000 equity in your home. Tax years in issue are 1984 through 1989. You were assessed $30,000 in 1990.

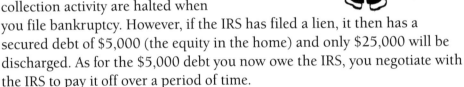

Solution:

You can discharge all of the tax debt by filing Chapter 7. The wage levy and collection activity are halted when you file bankruptcy. However, if the IRS has filed a lien, it then has a secured debt of $5,000 (the equity in the home) and only $25,000 will be discharged. As for the $5,000 debt you now owe the IRS, you negotiate with the IRS to pay it off over a period of time.

Discharging taxes through Chapter 13

If the tax debt meets the rules stated above, then it may also be discharged by filing Chapter 13. In addition, the tax may be discharged in Chapter 13 even if:

- no return was filed for the tax
- the tax claims were based upon a fraudulent return or there was willful intent to evade tax
- it is an unsecured, non-dischargeable tax, such as withholding or sales tax, when the IRS or New York State failed to file a timely proof of claim

Chapter 13 allows a greater number of options for a client than a Chapter 7. There are also several situations in which a Chapter 13 is useful in dealing with delinquent taxes:

1. When the Court confirms the Chapter 13 plan, taxes due to the IRS, New York State or a municipality (for back real estate taxes) may be paid over time ranging from 36 to 60 months and at a rate the individual can afford.

2. The Chapter 13 stops additional post-petition interest and penalties on tax debt due to the IRS and New York State where the claim is unsecured.

3. No assets need to be surrendered in Chapter 13.

Example:

The IRS has levied your wages and attached your bank account, claiming you owe $30,000 in back taxes, interest and penalties. You have an income of $25,000. You have $5,000 equity in your home. The IRS has filed a lien. Tax years in issue are 1985 through 1990. You have not filed returns at all for that period of time. You were assessed in 1991.

Solution:

When you file a Chapter 13 plan, $25,000 of the tax debt will be treated as unsecured — you will pay part or all of it back, depending on the amount of your income remaining after you pay normal living expenses. The wage levy and collection activities are halted when you file. The IRS has a secured claim of $5,000, which represents the equity in your home. A Chapter 13 plan could provide to pay that $5,000 to the IRS for 36 to 60 months, plus interest as required by law, depending on your income plus any other tax you have to pay.

What if the taxes cannot be discharged in Chapter 13 or Chapter 7? Let's say a client owes $6,000 of non-dischargeable taxes. We may propose a Chapter 13 plan and pay this debt in full over 60 months at $100 per month. In many cases no interest will be required at all, and once the case is filed, no additional penalties may be assessed.

Timing Is Crucial

People are often in a race to the courthouse with the IRS or New York State. If you file your bankruptcy petition before a lien is filed, that tax debt will not be secured, which could make a big difference. If the claim is secured, it is paid with interest; an unsecured claim is paid with no interest after the bankruptcy filing date. On the other hand, filing too early can prevent the discharge of the tax debt.

What chapter to choose?

Bankruptcy may provide a taxpayer with alternative methods for dealing with delinquent taxes if a satisfactory payment arrangement with the taxing authority cannot be reached. The tax issues involved in determining which chapter to choose are not limited to dischargeability. A careful analysis of all of the individual's taxes and debts by a qualified attorney will be required before a proper choice can be made.

One final note:
Beware of the IRS if you settle a debt — The forgiveness of debt outside of bankruptcy is imputed income

IRS rules could cost you a substantial amount of money if you settle debts outside of your bankruptcy. Any creditor that forgives your debt or a part of your debt for $600 or more must send you and the IRS a 1099-C form at the end of the year. The 1099-C is a report of income, which means that when you file your tax returns for the tax year in which your debt was forgiven, the IRS will check to make sure that you report the amount on the 1099-C as income.

Before making a settlement of a debt with a creditor outside of bankruptcy, have your accountant calculate your tax liability. If your tax bill will be too high, you may be better off filing Chapter 7 or Chapter 13 and discharging the entire debt.

17

How To Re-establish Credit

I never met a client whose credit was too terrible to rebuild. Your recent experience with financial problems might lead you to believe it will be impossible to obtain credit again. This is simply not true. After a few years, you should be able to re-establish your credit, enabling you to obtain a MasterCard, Visa or bank loan. Many lenders will grant credit to those who have put their financial houses in order.

Some creditors want you to believe you'll never get credit again. Bear in mind that if you're behind on your bills, your credit record is marked slow payments for six years and nine months whether you file bankruptcy or not. If you have slow pay listed on your credit record, bankruptcy will not make it significantly worse.

Credit will take time to rebuild

The Fair Credit Reporting Act permits a credit reporting organization to report Chapters 7 and 13 for 10 years. But most local credit reporting agencies list Chapter 7 bankruptcy on your credit report for nine years and nine months, and Chapter 13 for six years and nine months. This does not mean that you have to wait that long to re-establish your credit.

It's difficult to go through life without credit — you need it to rent a car and may need it to reserve a hotel room. But realize that credit may have played a big role in getting you into financial difficulties.

You may want to obtain some help with budgeting before you begin to re-establish credit. Consumer Credit Counseling can provide comprehensive budgeting programs through its educational services department at 546-3440. Some offices of the Cornell Cooperative Extension offer confidential financial counseling, budget counseling and advice on obtaining credit through its Family Budget Counseling Program. The staff is made up of trained counselors who provide their services free of charge. In Ontario County, the Cooperative Extension number is 394-3977. In Wayne County, the Cooperative Extension number is 331-8415. In both counties, the programs are open only to residents.

Once you are sure you can handle credit again, be an educated consumer.

Many clients can successfully re-establish their credit by following the steps on the following pages.

Our Clients Have Used These Tips To Re-establish Their Credit:

1. Keep one of your credit cards

If you do file bankruptcy but you have a credit card or a line of credit that does not have an outstanding balance, you don't have to list that creditor on your bankruptcy petition or in your Chapter 13 plan. The creditor, therefore, will not be notified of your filing. You can use the account responsibly, and in doing so, help rebuild a positive credit record.

2. Obtain a secured credit card

A secured credit card can be a good way of getting your credit profile back into shape. This type of credit card was specifically developed for the consumer who needs to re-establish credit or who lacks a credit history.

A secured card simply means that you leave a sum of money on deposit in a savings account as collateral with the bank supplying the card. This serves as a guarantee that you will make payments on the account. Often, after a good repayment history has been established, the collateral will be either partially or completely released. If used correctly, a secured credit card will be a great boost to your credit record and will prove that you can handle credit responsibly.

More than 100 banks nationwide now offer secured credit cards, which look like regular MasterCards and Visas.

There is no difference in spending power between a secured and a non-secured card; you will have the same charging privileges, wide acceptance and convenience offered by a conventional card. There may be, however, higher interest rates, higher annual fees and special application processing fees charged. Low-interest cards and those with no annual fees are just not available to those who have had credit problems.

Remember also, that just because you have enough money to put down on a deposit for a secured card, you don't automatically become approved. Banks handle applications for secured cards on an individual basis. Some banks require the bankruptcy to be completely discharged and all judgments and federal tax liens to be paid before they will consider your application. Generally, the banks require around $400 to $500 on deposit and proof that you have a job or another steady source of income.

After you've had a secured credit card for some time, most banks will review your account's performance and decide whether or not to increase your credit limit or to return your security deposit. If this does not happen automatically, you can request that the bank review your account.

You should also find out which credit bureaus will get reports on your account. It's important for future reference that your record go to all the major bureaus in your area.

You should do some bank card shopping before taking a secured Visa, MasterCard or other offering. Application fees and annual dues can range from $25 to more than $200, and there are some less reputable marketing firms that deal in "credit rebuilding" cards with very limited use.

See Appendix E for a list of banks offering secured credit cards and the requirements for getting the cards. Banks do change their policies frequently, so this information changes as time goes on. Individuals in a Chapter 13 plan may have difficulty obtaining a secured card – see information for Orchard Bank in Appendix E.

If You're In Chapter 13, Check On Your Debt

If you are in a Chapter 13 plan, you must obtain permission from the trustee or the bankruptcy judge before incurring new debt over $500. To ensure that your request is reasonable, consult your attorney.

---

3. Apply for credit

Sometimes it's easier to obtain a credit card from a department store or a gasoline company. They'll usually open your account with very low credit lines. If you start with one credit card, charge on it and pay the bill on time, other companies will issue you cards.

4. Lay-away plans

If local merchants do not extend you credit, they may allow you to make a purchase on a lay-a-way plan. One advantage of lay-a-way is that you don't pay interest. These purchases are generally not reported to a credit bureau. However, if you purchase an item on lay-a-way and make all the payments on time, the store may be willing to issue you a store credit card or store credit privileges.

5. Co-signers

Another way to re-establish credit is to have a co-signer. Co-signers can use the strength of their good credit to assist others in getting financing.

6. Passbook savings loan

You may also look into the option of obtaining a passbook savings loan. One way to rebuild your credit is to take some money you've saved and open a savings account. You ask the bank to give you a loan against the money in the account. If you obtain a passbook loan, make sure that the bank reports your loan payments to the credit bureau. This is important – the main reason you took out the loan was to rebuild your credit. If the bank doesn't report your payments to the credit bureau, there is no reason to take out the passbook savings loan.

7. Know your banker

Develop a working relationship with a local bank. A savings account and a checking account can help you improve your standing with creditors. Bank accounts are signs of stability in the eyes of many creditors. Try saving $5 or $10 weekly or as much as you can.

8. Pay rent and utilities on time

Always make a point to allow room in your budget so you can make your rent and utility payments on time. And make sure those payments show up on your credit record.

9. Get a steady job

Creditors look for stability – and a steady job helps to improve your credit standing. Employment will enable you to start saving and rebuilding.

10. Review your credit record

Obtain a copy of your credit report from your local credit reporting agency. Credit reports are important because they are used by organizations such as banks and department stores in order to evaluate you as a candidate for future credit.

The majority of the information on a credit file is your credit history. A file normally contains the names of your creditors, the type of account, when it was opened, whether you take 30, 60 or 90 days to pay, your credit limit, the original amount of the loan and your current balance. The file will also show if any of the accounts have been turned over to a collection agency or if you're disputing any charges. If you file bankruptcy, have a slow payment or a judgment, that will also appear on your record.

What is a credit reporting agency?

Credit bureaus are profit-making companies that collect and sell information regarding an individual's credit history. These credit bureaus sell their information to banks, credit card companies, department stores, etc. Three of the major credit bureaus are Equifax, Experion (formerly TRW) and Trans Union.

11. Correcting credit report errors and reporting positive information

Review your credit report carefully to be sure it is accurate. If there are any discrepancies between the report and your records, you should contact the credit reporting agency to have them cleared up. The creditor in question will be contacted by the agency regarding any dispute you may have.

Here's a sample dispute letter:

(Date)

Complaint Dept.
Name of Credit Bureau
Address

Dear Sir or Madam:

I am writing to dispute the following information in my file. The items I dispute are encircled on the attached copy of the report I received.

This item is (inaccurate or incomplete) *because* (describe what is inaccurate and why). *I am requesting that the item be deleted* (or request another change) *to correct the information. Enclosed are copies* (use this sentence if you have documentation) *supporting my position.*

Please reinvestigate this matter and (delete or correct) *the disputed items as soon as possible.*

> *Sincerely*
> *Your Name*

Enclosures (list of materials you're enclosing)

The credit bureau will send you a form. They should respond to the form you filled out in 30 days. If disputed information cannot be verified, then it must be deleted from your record; if it is an error, it must be corrected.

It is important to put as much positive information on your credit record as possible. For example, make sure all positive account histories are on your credit record. Sometimes department store accounts, which could help your credit record if you have a steady payment record, are not reported — check with the bureau to see if these can be added.

If your credit file is missing credit histories for accounts you pay on time, send the credit bureau a copy of a recent account statement or a copy of canceled checks showing your payment history. Request the credit bureau to add the information to your file. Although the bureaus are not required to do so, they may oblige.

You may also consider adding your employment status, ownership of a residence, or checking and savings account information (however, you won't want to add the latter if you've been sued by a creditor or you think a creditor may sue you).

Check on your credit report to make sure your new, good credit is being reported

Make sure your date of birth is on your record. A lender will probably not grant you credit if it does not know your age. Especially add your age if you are over 50. People over 50 tend to be low credit risks and their incomes are usually higher than those under 50.

Check on your credit report every once in a while to make sure your new, good credit is being reported accurately. Many lenders are more interested in what you are doing now than in what you did in the past.

To avoid mix-ups on your credit report, follow these simple rules:
- Always use the same name when applying for credit; if you use a middle initial, or a "junior," use it consistently;
- Provide your Social Security number on applications
- List all your addresses over the last five years on applications, if possible
- If you have held many credit accounts jointly with your spouse, make sure you have a credit history in your own name, too
- Keep copies of all your correspondence with the credit bureau

If you have received a discharge in bankruptcy, make sure the credit bureau has a copy of your schedules showing which debts have been discharged. The records should show that you are no longer responsible for those debts.

Avoid Credit Repair Clinics

The advertisements make it sound like a cinch. "Need a loan because you have too many bills to pay? Can't get one because you have too many bills to pay? Solve all your problems with one call to this 900 number, for the small fee of $35!" And so on.

Credit repair clinics advertise that they can fix your credit and qualify you for a loan or a credit card. These clinics will not be able to do anything that you cannot do yourself, especially when it comes to obtaining a secured credit card or correcting information on your credit record.

In addition, many of the practices of the credit repair clinics are illegal. For example, one illegal practice involves obtaining the Social Security number of a deceased individual and substituting it for a person who has a poor credit history. These illegal schemes should be avoided at all costs.

Financial difficulties don't happen overnight, and they don't get solved overnight. It also doesn't help someone who is already burdened with debt to incur a $35 phone bill trying to get a loan that may be overloaded with initiation fees and interest charges.

12. Neutralize negative credit information: tell your side of the story

Sometimes there are negative items on your report that cannot be removed. In these cases, according to the Fair Credit Reporting Act, you are legally entitled to have a statement of up to 100 words attached to the report to neutralize bad information. For example:

"As a result of circumstances beyond our control, several years ago my wife and I were forced into a Chapter 13 plan. We filed Chapter 13 because we insisted on paying back every penny owed to all creditors. In less than three years, we paid off the entire $20,000 we owed. This demonstrates that we are responsible, and are good credit risks. We urge prospective creditors to bear this in mind when considering us for credit."

Remember that banks and stores evaluate your credit report differently, and will determine your eligibility for credit on a case-by-case basis.

Also, not all lenders have hard and fast rules about lending to someone who has filed Chapter 7 or 13. Some will take into consideration the merits of your case; for example, obligations you had to assume as the result of divorce or overwhelming medical expenses.

Requesting your report

You are entitled to get a copy of your credit file, and it's free in certain circumstances. If you have been denied credit within the past 30 days, you are eligible for a free credit report, according to the Fair Credit Reporting Act (although some of the reporting agencies extend the time frame to 60 days). If you don't qualify for a free report, the cost is $8. Depending on your credit history, you may want to consider obtaining your report from all the bureaus to check on the consistency of the information.

Contact the following bureaus for your credit report:

> The Credit Bureau, 19 Prince St.
> Rochester, NY 14607 — Phone: 256-8800
> (This is a local Equifax affiliate. They will answer questions pertaining to your credit report over the phone or in person at their office. There is no charge for this assistance.)

> Equifax Consumer Assistance Dept. (national office)
> PO Box 74041, Atlanta, GA 30374-0241
> Phone: 1-800-685-1111

> Experion (formerly TRW) National Consumer Assistance Center
> Box 949, Allen, TX 75002-0949 — Phone:1-800-682-7654

> Trans Union — Phone: 1-800-632-1765
> Credit Bureau Services Regional Service Center

When you request a copy of your report, you will need to include your full name, address, previous addresses during the last five years, Social Security number, date of birth, spouse's first name and a photocopy of a billing statement or driver's license that links your name with your mailing address.

For more information

The Federal Trade Commission produces a series of pamphlets on credit issues, such as detailed information on how to dispute information in a credit report. These pamphlets include:

> *Building a Better Credit Record*
> *Credit and Divorce*
> *Credit Billing Errors*
> *Fair Credit Billing*
> *Fair Credit Reporting*
> *Fair Debt Collection*
> *Fix Your Own Credit Problems*
> *Solving Credit Problems*
> *Women and Credit Histories*

To obtain free copies of this information contact: **Public Reference, Federal Trade Commission, Washington, DC 20580.**

Credit Rehabilitation For Chapter 13 Debtors

The Chapter 13 Trustee's office in Rochester runs "credit rehabilitation" classes for Chapter 13 debtors. For more information on the sessions, contact the trustee's office at 427-7225.

---

13. Applying for a mortgage

Eventually, you may be in the position of applying for a mortgage after you've made significant strides in re-establishing your credit.

Although you will have to meet more criteria to qualify for a home mortgage than you would have if you had not filed bankruptcy, it is still possible to purchase a home. If you are in a position to make regular mortgage payments, you may want to consider purchasing a home and obtaining a mortgage as part of a plan to continue rebuilding your financial status.

Appendix C gives a list of banks willing to consider mortgage applicants who have previously filed bankruptcy. Banks will often offer FHA mortgages to post-bankruptcy applicants because they are easier to obtain.

Be aware that lenders review mortgage applications on a case-by-case basis. Many factors will enter into this review process.

When applying for a mortgage, be prepared to answer questions about why your bankruptcy was filed and provide proof that bills such as rent and utilities have been paid consistently following the bankruptcy. It is also helpful if you make regular contributions to a savings account and to have a reserve in the bank equal to three or four mortgage payments, particularly if you apply for a conventional (not FHA or VA) loan.

If you've had a previous home foreclosure, you may encounter more difficulty in obtaining approval for a loan unless you can show good reasons for the foreclosure (such as job loss or medical problems).

A credit success story

Here's one example of how credit was successfully re-established following a bankruptcy:

Just a few years after filing Chapter 7 bankruptcy, Jane began taking steps to re-establish her credit. Besides dealing with the various aspects of her debt problems, she also spent many years overcoming the stigma of filing a case with the bankruptcy court. She was embarrassed that she worked so hard, yet still was forced to file bankruptcy due to her overwhelming debt.

In 1989, Jane filed Chapter 7 following a layoff and an extended illness. She had a large number of medical bills, and lost her medical insurance following the layoff. When she filed for bankruptcy, she was able to keep her car and all her personal belongings such as furniture, appliances, clothes, etc. She gave up three credit cards. She was relieved of $25,000 in debt and also $15,000 in medical bills. Shortly after the filing, she found a job as a salesperson.

In 1990, her sales improved and she obtained a nice raise. She deposited $800 in a savings account and obtained a secured credit card. She used the card and paid in a timely fashion, which is a very important key to re-establishing credit. During the year, Jane reviewed her credit report to make sure her payment history was being recorded.

In 1991, Jane's credit card was converted from secured to a regular card. Her $800 deposit that was needed for the secured card was returned.

At the end of 1991, Jane bought a home. She learned that she could obtain an FHA mortgage just two years after bankruptcy.

In 1992, Jane borrowed $3,500 to buy a used car, and a friend co-signed. That same year, she received a bonus at work and paid off the loan.

Although the bankruptcy will not be removed from Jane's credit record until 1999, she has made many advances in re-establishing her credit, with a credit card, a house and a car.

We continue to revise the materials we distribute to clients regarding credit. If you'd like to share your credit rebuilding tips, send your story to us at: Jeffrey Freedman Attorneys at Law, 1577 Ridge Road W., Rochester, NY 14615. Your information may be very helpful to another individual in similar circumstances.

18

Hiring A Bankruptcy Attorney

Hiring a lawyer to handle a legal matter is a difficult process, especially when you are under stress.

When you are hiring a professional to assist you, it is vitally important to select someone who will be responsive to your needs. The lawyer should not be too busy to meet with you individually and answer questions that may arise. You should take care before you retain an attorney to meet the attorney personally, and be sure you can relate to the attorney's method of dealing with your situation.

From the time you retain the attorney until the matter is finally completed, the lawyer or the paralegals on the staff should be able to answer your questions in a timely fashion. Before you retain the attorney ask him or her how long will it take to have calls returned should you have a question.

Under what circumstances would you need a lawyer?

If you are unfamiliar with the procedures involved, or if there may be negative repercussions that follow from what you do, consult an attorney. In many situations, people try to "do it themselves" and find out later they made a big mistake. Bankruptcy law is very complex and there are many pitfalls involved.

Lawyers Fees

What are typical rates for lawyers?

Fees vary according to the law firm's expertise. If your case is being handled on an hourly basis, a retainer agreement will specify the hourly fee for the attorneys and paralegals working on your case. Retainers and other documents should be read carefully before you sign them. A partner in a law firm may charge $175 per hour, where an associate may charge $125 per hour, and a paralegal $75 per hour. Carefully read and understand the retainer agreement before signing it. It is a contract between lawyer and client.

What is a paralegal?

A paralegal is a legal assistant who works under the supervision of attorneys, and helps the attorneys serve clients. This individual may help draft papers, interview clients, and prepare cases for court. The paralegal is qualified through either education or work experience to assist in serving clients.

What are the typical hourly rates for paralegals?

The rates are generally less than half that of the supervising attorney's fee for cases billed on an hourly basis. By using paralegals, many law firms are able to keep legal fees down and serve their clients in a more economical manner.

Conclusion

One of the best ways to find a good bankruptcy attorney is to obtain recommendations from friends and family. And remember, as in all areas of life, you get what you pay for. The lawyer with the cheapest rate is not necessarily the best.

19

Conclusion

Fortunately for all of us, there are no longer debtor's prisons in America. In some countries today, if you don't pay your bills, you go to jail. This does not happen in America because our system helps people who are in over their heads. We have a safety release by virtue of our laws which give you the right to file for bankruptcy.

It is important to know that if you are already behind on your bills before you file for bankruptcy, your credit record is marked for seven years anyway. Filing Chapter 13 will go on your credit record for six years and nine months, or filing a Chapter 7 straight bankruptcy will remain on your record for nine years and nine months. By filing bankruptcy you are released from a substantial portion of your debt.

Most of my clients who decide to file for bankruptcy previously made a good faith effort to repay their debts. For some there was no way out other than to file for bankruptcy. Financial problems may be the result of a job loss, matrimonial problems, a serious illness, an accident, poor budgeting or overspending. Regardless of the reason, you have a legal right protected by federal law to file for bankruptcy.

A lawyer who is familiar with the bankruptcy process can help you understand your options and help you decide what the best course of action is for you and your family.

20

Definition Of Terms

Answer: A pleading in a civil case, in which the Defendant responds to the Plaintiff's complaint.

Attachment: The seizure of another's property according to a judicial order. The attachment and sale of property is one method for collecting a money judgment.

Bankruptcy: A legal procedure that allows a debtor to free himself or herself of debt.

Chapter 7: Gives the debtor a fresh start without repaying part or all of his or her debt.

Chapter 13: Frees the debtor from creditor harassment and allows him or her to keep all property, while attempting to partially or entirely repay debts over a three- to five-year period.

Complaint: In civil procedure, a pleading that is the written statement by the Plaintiff of the facts on which a cause of action is based.

Constitution: The written document that is the fundamental law. The U.S. Constitution is the fundamental law of the nation. The New York State Constitution is the fundamental law of the state.

Co-signer: A person who signs on a loan for another person, thus personally guaranteeing the debt will be repaid. If the debtor chooses to discharge the debt in a Chapter 7 bankruptcy, the co-signer becomes responsible for it.

Creditor: The person who has loaned the money.

Court Docket Sheet: A chronological summary of the history of the bankruptcy or Chapter 13 case. This may be obtained from the bankruptcy court clerk's office.

Debt: A legal obligation to pay money.

Default: In civil procedure, a failure to file a pleading within the time allowed, or failure to appear in court when required. Except in certain instances, final judgment may be entered against a party in default, without trial.

Defendant: The party against whom a civil action is brought.

Discharge: The legal forgiveness of a debt, given by a bankruptcy judge.

Dischargeable Debt: A debt that can be forgiven in a bankruptcy.

Equity: The value of property less any debts owed against that property.

Exempt Property: Property that a debtor is allowed to keep after a bankruptcy. Married couples filing jointly can each claim a full set of exemptions.

File: To begin bankruptcy proceedings by filling out the appropriate forms, paying the filing fee and filing the bankruptcy petition in the Bankruptcy Court.

Foreclosure: A type of legal proceeding taken to enforce payment of a debt through the sale of property against which the creditor holds a lien.

Forms: The petition, schedule of property, list of exemptions, list of creditors, a budget including income and expenses, and personal information; all the forms which must be filled out and filed with the bankruptcy clerk to begin bankruptcy proceedings.

Garnishment: A type of legal proceeding taken to enforce payment of a debt, in which property of the debtor is taken (i.e. wage garnishment).

Homestead: The family home, if you are a homeowner. Part or even all of the equity in the homestead is exempt property up to $10,000 per debtor.

Judgment:	A final order of a trial court, which gives effect to the decision in the case.
Lien:	Any of a variety of charges or encumbrances on property imposed to secure the payment of a debt or the performance or non-performance of an act. Liens are enforced by some type of foreclosure proceeding. Liens can be imposed on real property or personal property.
Liquidation Value:	The forced sale value of property, similar to the price you would get if you auctioned the property, or sold it at a pawn shop, flea market or yard sale.
Meeting of Creditors/341 Meeting:	The meeting which takes place approximately one month after the bankruptcy filing, during which the trustee asks the debtor questions about his or her property.
Nondischargeable Debt:	A debt that cannot be wiped out in bankruptcy, such as some income taxes.
Nonexempt Property:	The property a debtor must surrender to the bankruptcy trustee, who uses it to pay the debtor's creditors.
Plaintiff:	The complaining party in a civil action.
Property:	All of the debtor's possessions.
Retail Installment Sale:	A type of retail sale of retail goods with payment to be made in a series of installments. Retail installment sales are regulated by statute in New York.
Secured Debt:	A debt which is backed up by some property. For instance with an automobile loan, the car offers security for the loan. If the loan is not repaid, the lender can repossess the car.

Security Interest: A lien on property, acquired pursuant to a written agreement to secure repayment of a loan or other debt.

The Trustee's Report of Receipts and Disbursements: This is a document that summarizes payments that a Chapter 13 debtor has made to the trustee. It also shows the payments that the trustee has made to various creditors. This document is sent to the debtor in November and in May. However, the debtor may obtain a copy every month from the trustee.

Trustee: The person who takes charge of a bankruptcy; he or she sells the debtor's nonexempt property and divides the sales proceeds among the creditors. In most cases all property is exempt and therefore the trustee has nothing to sell. The trustee also reviews the bankruptcy petition and examines debtors under oath. In a Chapter 13 the trustee collects money from the debtor and pays the creditors over a three- to five-year period.

Unsecured Debt: Obligations based purely on the debtor's future ability to pay. For example: doctor's bills, VISA charges and department store charges.

Appendix A

Chapter 13 Plans — Sample #1

A Typical Chapter 13 Plan

Name: Harvey Needleman

Balance of attorney fees to be paid in the Plan	$ 500
Priority debt	none
Mortgage arrears	none
Automobile loan #1, $8,000 at 9% interest for 60 months . .	$ 9,500
Automobile loan #2	none
Co-signed debt	none
Miscellaneous debt	none
Unsecured debt, $31,000 x 5% = ...	$ 1,500
Trustee's commission = 7.5%	$ 860
Total of all funds to be paid through the Chapter 13 Plan . .	$12,360
Number of months the plan will last	60
Total amount to be paid each month	$ 206
Debtor or debtor's employer shall pay to the trustee the sum of . . . . on a weekly basis	$ 48

Mr. Needleman has an income of $2,500 per month and expenses totaling $2,294 per month. He owns a 1992 Chevrolet with a fair market value of $8,000. The balance due to the bank on the car is $15,000. His house has a fair market value of $80,000 with a mortgage of $70,000. The equity in the home is exempt.

Mr. Needleman owes $4,000 in medical bills and $20,000 to VISA.

If he filed Chapter 7, Mr. Needleman would pay $15,000 plus interest to the car creditor, by making the regular payments. His credit record is marked for 9 years and 9 months.

If he filed Chapter 13, Mr. Needleman would obtain the vehicle for $8,000 plus interest and would pay this within the plan over 3-5 years.

His credit record is marked for 6 years and 9 months by filing Chapter 13.

If Mr. Needleman wants to keep his home, he must make the mortgage payments in Chapter 7 or Chapter 13.

Chapter 13 Plan – Sample #2

Property Protection Method

Name: Ramona Rifkin

Balance of attorney fees to be paid in the Plan . . . .$	500
Priority debt	none
Mortgage arrears	none
Automobile loan # 1	none
Automobile loan #2	none
Co-signed debt	none
Miscellaneous debt	none
Unsecured debt $10,000 x 50% = ...$	5,000
Trustee's commission = 7.5% . . . .$	412
Total of all funds to be paid through the Chapter 13 Plan . . . .$	5,912
Number of months that the plan will last	36
Total amount to be paid each month . . . .$	165
Debtor or debtor's employer shall pay to the trustee the sum of . . . .$ on a weekly basis	39

Ms. Rifkin owes $ 10,000 in debt, all unsecured: doctor bills, store charges and VISA debt. She owns a cottage but she does not reside there, so this asset is not exempt under state or federal law. The cottage has a value of $5,000 more than the mortgage on it.

Note: If Ms. Rifkin filed Chapter 7, the trustee would sell the cottage and the creditors would get $5,000 or 50 percent of what is owed. If, however, she files Chapter 13, she must offer her unsecured creditors at least $.50 on the dollar. Debtors with a fair amount of non-exempt property lose it in Chapter 7, or they pay the equivalent value of the property to their creditors in Chapter 13.

Thus, Ms. Rifkin's plan would pay 50% of unsecured claims over a term of three years. Nine percent interest would also be paid while the plan is in effect. If she needed a lower payment plan, the plan could go for five years at $99 per month.

Chapter 13 Plan — Sample #3

100% Method

Name: Harvey Needleman

Balance of attorney fees to be paid in Plan	$	500
Priority debt		none
Mortgage arrears		none
Automobile loan #1 $8,000 at 9% interest for 60 mos.	$	9,500
Automobile loan #2		none
Co-signed debt		none
Miscellaneous secured debt		none
Unsecured debt $31,000 x 100% = ...	$	31,000
Trustee's commission = 7.5%	$	3,000
Total of all funds to be paid through the Chapter 13 Plan . .	$	44,000
Number of months plan will last		60
Total amount to be paid each month	$	733
Debtor or debtor's employer shall pay to the trustee the sum of.	$	170
on a weekly basis		

Note: This plan is the same as Plan #1, except that the client wants to pay creditors 100% of the debt he owes them. Mr. Needleman needs additional income of $527 per month in order to fulfill this plan and he will get a part time job to earn the extra income so he can afford the 100% plan.

Chapter 13 Plan — Sample #4

Save The Home From Foreclosure

Name: Seymour Sidesaddle

Balance of attorney fees to be paid in the Plan . . . . $ 500

Priority debt (real estate taxes $1,000 x 9% x 36 months) . . $ 1,100

Mortgage arrears $3,000 x 9% interest x 36 months . . . . $ 3,400

Automobile loan #1 FMV $4,000 x 9% interest x 36 months $ 5,000

Automobile loan #2 . . . .   none

Co-signed debt . . . .   none

Miscellaneous debt . . . .   none

Unsecured debt $24,000 x 20% = ... $ 4,800

Trustee's commission = 7.5% . . . . $ 1,110

Total of all funds to be paid through the Chapter 13 Plan . . $ 15,910

Number of months that the plan will last   36

Total amount to be paid each month . . . . $ 442

Debtor or debtor's employer shall
pay the sum of . . . . $ 103
to the trustee on a weekly basis

Note: Mr. Sidesaddle has a net income of $2,200 per month. His expenses are $1,758 per month. He owns a car valued at $4,000 with a lien of $8,000 and real estate worth $70,000 which has a mortgage of $60,000. The equity in the real estate is exempt. Unfortunately, Mr. Sidesaddle has fallen behind on his mortgage payments by approximately $3,000. He also owes his attorney $500 to process the Chapter 13 case and has $20,000 in unsecured debts.

Chapter 13 will allow Mr. Sidesaddle to keep his home, car and other property. It will allow him to work with his creditors, in a manner he can afford.

Chapter 13 Plan – Sample #5

I Want To Save My Business

Name: Ms. Shelby Hamilton

Balance of attorney fees to be paid in the Plan	$ 1,000
Priority debt (Sales tax)	$10,000
Mortgage arrearages	none
Automobile loan #1	none
Automobile loan #2	none
Co-signed debt	none
Miscellaneous debt	none
Unsecured debt $60,000 x 10% = ...	$ 6,000
Interest to be paid to creditors in the plan at 9% per annum	$ 2,500
Trustee's commission = 7.5%	$ 1,400
Total of all funds to be paid through the Chapter 13 Plan . .	$21,000
Number of months the plan will last	60
Total amount to be paid each month to the trustee	$ 350

Shelby Hamilton's pet supply store has run into financial problems. Shelby thinks that it is only a temporary situation. The State of New York believes the problem is very serious and threatens to close down the store due to delinquent taxes any day now.

Ms. Hamilton has unsecured personal and business debt of approximately $60,000. She also owes New York State $10,000 for past due sales taxes. She estimates that the liquidation value of her business assets is $16,000. All of her personal assets are exempt.

Shelby Hamilton estimates that if she could somehow deal with her creditors, she might be able to make a profit in her business and net $2,800 per month.

To support her family and pay household expenses and current income taxes, Ms. Hamilton needs $2,250 per month.

If Ms. Hamilton filed Chapter 7 and her business assets were liquidated, the net proceeds after the auction would be $16,000. Priority debt (sales tax) would be paid in full; and unsecured creditors would get a 10% dividend, or $6,000.

If Ms. Hamilton wants to remain in business, she could file a Chapter 13 re-organization. Her Chapter 13 plan would be required to meet the following tests in order to be approved by the judge:

1. Priority debt must be paid in full ($10,000 to NYS)

2. Unsecured creditors must receive at least what they would be entitled to receive if the debtor filed Chapter 7 ($6,000).

3. The debtor must pay into the plan as much as her budget would allow for at least 3 years.

4. The plan must be filed in good faith.

Filing a chapter 13 plan by Shelby would stop all creditors, including New York State, from taking action and would allow her to remain in business.

The Bankruptcy Code grants the bankruptcy judge a great deal of discretion whether or not a plan will be approved. As a condition of confirmation, it may be required that a plan extend for up to 60 months.

Appendix B

The General Shut-off Policies Of Utility Companies

At this writing, the following information represents the shut-off policies of utilities.

Rochester Gas & Electric

For answers to questions pertaining to shut-offs, payment problems, extensions or how bankruptcy will affect your service, call the utility direct at 546-1111.

Niagara Mohawk

If your account is delinquent, the knowledge that you intend to file bankruptcy will not delay a shut-off with Niagara Mohawk. If your service is already off, it will not be reinstated until after you have filed your petition.

You or your attorney should write or phone the company to inform them you have filed and to ask them to reinstate service. The attorney's office must have your correct account number in order to do this, along with the case number, date of filing, chapter, court, etc.

Niagara Mohawk will always require a security deposit if they are listed on your petition. Generally, the amount required must not exceed two times the average monthly bill for a calendar year except in the case of electric heat customers, where deposits must not exceed two times the estimated average monthly bill for the heating season.

If you cannot pay the total deposit at once, Niagara Mohawk may enter into an Installment Agreement with you. As long as you maintain the terms of this agreement and pay all bills in a timely manner after your bankruptcy filing, your service will not be shut off.

Rochester Telephone

If you plan to file bankruptcy, it is important to list the phone company as a creditor. Rochester Telephone may require a security deposit following the bankruptcy if you plan to continue phone service or need to re-establish phone service if you've been disconnected.

Each case is reviewed on an individual basis. If you have questions regarding payment problems, disconnect notices or how to continue service following bankruptcy, call Rochester Telephone at 777-1270.

Summary

All utility companies can request a security deposit. They cannot ask you to pay the past due balance before they reinstate service or stop a shut-off.

If the security deposit will be higher than the bill owed, it is best to pay off the bill, and you will not be responsible for the security deposit.

When you speak with the utility company to arrange your security deposit, ask them what you will have to do to get it back. Usually, after a certain amount of on-time payments, or the life of your Chapter 13 plan, they will return that money to you. This changes from case to case, so you must ask about the requirements for your situation.

Special protections apply for those who are disabled

Anyone who is blind, or otherwise disabled, is protected by the Home Energy Fair Practices Act against a shut-off of gas, electric or steam service, according to the Public Service Commission (PSC). This act gives you protection against shut-offs, restrictions on deposits and the right to a payment plan.

If your utility service is for heat and you are in danger of a shut-off during the cold weather protection period (November 1 to April 15), you must be contacted by phone or in person 72 hours before the scheduled shut-off.

You will also be contacted in person at the time of the scheduled shut-off to find out if you or someone in your household would be likely to suffer a serious health or safety problem as a result of the shut-off. If this is the case, your service will not be shut off and the utility will notify the Department of Social Services.

Those who depend on a utility to operate life support equipment such as a dialysis machine or respirator can get certification from their doctor or the local Board of Health. The service will remain on as long as the equipment is needed.

Telephone service can be limited in two ways if you have not paid your bills. With a suspension you can phone out but cannot receive phone calls. If you have been shut-off you cannot make or receive calls. Those who are disabled have 28 days after notification before service is suspended; and 40 days after notification before service is shut off. Other customers have only eight days after notification before service is suspended and 20 days before a shut-off.

Agreements and deposits

If you have become overdue on your utility bills, the company must give you time to pay the overdue amount in installments. This option must be offered at least five days before the shut-off, and must be fair. If you can't reach a satisfactory agreement with your utility company, call the Public Service Commission's HOTLINE at 1-800-342-3355.

You only have to miss two payments in a row to be asked for a deposit from your utility company unless you are a senior citizen or receive public assistance. The amount of deposit will depend on your utility company (see above), and you can pay it over a 12-month period. If you pay your bills on time for one year, your deposit will be refunded.

Utility companies will send credit and shut-off notices to a third person who is a friend or relative, as long as he or she agrees in writing to receive the notices. This person would not be responsible for paying your bill, but would make sure you realize you owe money and are in danger of having your service shut-off.

Complaints

If you are having problems with your service or with paying your bill, call your utility company first. If you can't work things out, contact the New York State Public Service Commission (PSC) HELPLINE at 1-800-342-3377 for assistance.

While the PSC is investigating, you may pay only the portion of your bill that is not in dispute and your service will not be disrupted. The PSC will notify you of the decision on your complaint. If you are not satisfied you have 15 days to ask for an informal hearing or informal review. You can appeal once more to the PSC within 15 days of the hearing to review the decision if you are still not satisfied.

For those utility customers who have special needs (senior citizens, blind, disabled and low income) the PSC has initiated a new priority service by designating a statewide ombudsperson. The ombudsperson processes complaints on a high priority basis and also provides general consumer assistance.

> You only have to miss two payments in a row to be asked for a deposit from your utility company

Appendix C

Mortgage Lenders For The Post-bankruptcy Borrower

Some bankruptcy clients have contacted the following organizations for assistance in obtaining mortgages. As with all recommendations in this publication, you are encouraged to do your own research. Lender policies regarding mortgages may be subject to change. There are other local lenders not listed here who will grant mortgages to individuals who have filed for bankruptcy. You can find these lenders through the phone book or by contacting your bank.

Brentwood Mortgage
6800 Pittsford Palmyra Road – Suite 220
Fairport, NY 14450
425-2507
1-800-724-7407

Mortgage requirements: Brentwood Mortgage is a Rochester-based company that specializes in obtaining mortgages for individuals who have encountered financial difficulties.

Each case is reviewed on an individual basis. Most mortgages, including FHA and VA, are obtained after Chapter 7 and Chapter 13 have been discharged for two years. However, it is possible for some individuals to obtain mortgages after one year.

Brentwood will work with individuals in a Chapter 13 plan, and pay off the outstanding balance. In addition, Brentwood has programs to grant mortgages one day after the bankruptcy has been discharged.

ESL Federal Credit Union
100 Kings Highway S. – Suite 1200
Rochester, NY 14617
1-800-848-2265 or 716-724-1510

Mortgage requirements: If you are a Kodak employee or retiree, or family member of an employee or retiree, you can contact ESL for more information on a variety of mortgage products. Each mortgage application is handled on an individual basis. Basically, ESL will look for re-established credit, stability and the reason for the bankruptcy. If you are not a member of this credit union, you must apply for membership before you are eligible for a mortgage loan.

Intercounty Mortgage Inc.
650 Clinton Square
Rochester, NY 14604
546-6260
1-800-581-4264

Mortgage requirements: To qualify for FHA, a Chapter 7 bankruptcy must be discharged for two years. Less than two years but more than 12 months may also be acceptable if the borrower can prove the bankruptcy was caused by circumstances beyond his or her control, and the situation is not likely to occur again. Re-established credit and ability to manage financial affairs need to be demonstrated.

For VA loans, a Chapter 7 bankruptcy needs to be discharged for at least two years. Borrowers need to prove steady employment, have re-established credit and proof that the bankruptcy was caused by circumstances beyond the control of the borrower.

To qualify for FHA following Chapter 13, the borrower may qualify if one year of the payback period has elapsed, performance has been satisfactory and court approval is received from the trustee. After the plan is complete, a letter from the trustee is still required.

For VA loans, payments to the Chapter 13 plan must be made satisfactorily and credit re-established. If applicants apply for a loan before the completion of the plan, favorable consideration may be given if at least three-fourths of the payments have been made satisfactorily and the trustee approves.

M&T Mortgage Corporation
One Fountain Plaza
Buffalo, NY 14203
848-4848

Mortgage requirements: At M&T, all loans are reviewed on an individual basis. M&T offers a full range of mortgage programs, including conventional fixed rate mortgages as well as affordable loans, such as FHA, VA and other government loans. M&T usually requires that both Chapter 7 and Chapter 13 bankruptcies be discharged two years prior to applying for a loan. M&T offers a series of informational brochures on "Understanding Loans and Credit," including how to improve a credit rating, how to establish a credit history and steps to loan approval.

Norwest Mortgage Inc.
1 John James Audubon Pkwy.
Amherst, NY 14228
Contact: Frank Sardina
1-800-759-7912

Mortgage requirements: All loans are reviewed on a case-by-case basis. Most loans to post-bankruptcy borrowers are FHA and VA loans.

General guidelines to qualify for FHA and VA loans following Chapter 7:
• the bankruptcy must be discharged for two years
• the applicant must have a letter explaining the reasons for the bankruptcy
• the applicant must have some record of re-established credit, with no delinquencies

General guidelines to qualify for FHA and VA loans following Chapter 13:
• the applicant must be in the Chapter 13 plan for at least one year
• a letter from the Chapter 13 trustee must be received, stating approval for the loan
• the applicant must provide a letter explaining reasons for the bankruptcy

United Companies Lending Corporation
6225 Sheridan Drive
Building C – Suite 302
Amherst, NY 14221
Contact: Mark O'Connell
633-3753

Mortgage requirements: All loans are reviewed on a case-by-case basis. UCLC is able to work with individuals immediately after filing a Chapter 7 as well as those still paying on a Chapter 13 plan. The company is a non-conforming mortgage lender that serves people who need a first or second mortgage and do not qualify under traditional mortgage lending parameters. UCLC is able to originate loans for debt consolidation, home improvements or new purchases. UCLC stresses service to the client and will meet with you at your home to discuss the options available to you.

Appendix D

Auto Loans For The Post-bankruptcy Borrower

Bob Johnson Chevrolet (used cars only)
1110 Stone Road
Rochester, NY 14616
Phone: 663-4470

Requirements: Six months residency, six months of steady employment and a net paycheck of at least $160/week. Down payments range from 12 to 33 percent of the price of the vehicle. Available cars are generally 5 to 8 years old. Bankruptcies must be discharged, and a copy of the discharge must be provided if the bankruptcy occurred in the last three years.

Charity Auto Inc. (used cars only)
111 Lake Ave.
Rochester, NY 14608
Phone: 254-6500

Requirements: Bankruptcies must be discharged, proof of residency provided and net paycheck of at least $150/week. Down payment required of at least $500. Available cars range from 3 to 10 years old, with one year warranty.

Cortese Dodge/Suzuki
2400 W. Henrietta Road
Rochester, NY 14623
Phone: 424-3000, ext. 151
Contact: Patrick Mullen

Requirements: Any bankruptcy not discharged must have a letter from the trustee. Financing is available but may require higher down payment for bankruptcies discharged for less than a year. Proof of residence and job stability are important. Each application reviewed on a case-by-case basis.

Marina Dodge

65 Pattonwood Dr.
Rochester, NY 14617
Phone: 342-5000
Contact: Peter Montante

Requirements: Recent bankruptcy filers need to present proof of employment and residence for one year, and proof of income of at least $1,200/month. The dealer will also ask for references.

Webster Chrysler-Jeep

2111 Empire Blvd.
Webster, NY 14580
Phone: 671-1010

Requirements: Bankruptcy must be discharged, with proof of steady work and residency in the last five years.

Other Sources of Auto Loans:

ESL Federal Credit Union

100 Kings Highway S. — Suite 1200
Rochester, NY 14617
Phone: 1-800-848-2265 or 716-724-1510

If you are a Kodak employee or retiree, or family member of an employee or retiree, you can contact ESL for more information on a variety of auto loan products. Each application is handled on an individual basis. Basically, ESL will look for re-established credit, stability and the reason for the bankruptcy. If you are not a member of this credit union, you must apply for membership before you are eligible for a loan.

Rochester Used Car Dealers Association
99 Edgemoor Rd.
Rochester, NY 14618
Phone: 244-8800
Contact: Stewart Winston

This association represents used car dealers in the Rochester area. It provides information on auto loans for individuals with a history of financial problems and offers listings on available used cars in its dealer network. The association also helps to match available used cars with the buyer's preferences and financial ability.

Important points to remember:

1. Keep in mind that approvals for auto loans are handled on an individual basis. Interest rates and minimum down payments can vary widely, so do your homework before you buy!

2. If you are in a Chapter 13 plan, you need to obtain permission from the trustee or the bankruptcy judge prior to incurring any new debts over $500. Consult your attorney prior to borrowing to be certain all court rules are followed.

Appendix E

Sources Of Secured Credit Cards

These sources of secured credit cards appear in alphabetical order. Some of our clients have contacted the following firms and some have had success depending on their situations. However, there are many more sources of secured cards and we encourage you to contact the organizations mentioned at the end of this chapter for a complete listing.

Also, be aware that requirements and fees can change. Use the information here only as a guideline.

Capital One

Card offered: Visa and MasterCard

Annual Percentage Rate: 19.6%

Fees: Depends on the program requested

Deposit: $200 minimum
(if you don't have $200, send in as much money as you can spare and account will begin earning interest immediately; once $200 minimum is reached, card is issued)

Account Type: Savings account will earn 4.89% interest rate

Grace period: 25 days

Review period: After 1 year, you may receive partially unsecured increase

Address: PO Box 85018
          Richmond, VA 23285-5018

Phone: 1-800-333-7116

Community Bank of Parker

Card offered: Visa

Annual Percentage Rate: 14.9%

Fees: $35

Deposit: $500 minimum

Account type: Savings with no interest

Grace period: 25 days

Review period: After 1 year, apply for unsecured increase

Address: Community Bank of Parker
          19590 E. Main St.
          Parker, CO 80134

Phone: 1-800-779-8472

First National Bank

Card offered: Visa and MasterCard

Annual Percentage Rate:
   16.9% on balances over $1,000; 18.9% on balances under $1,000

Fees: $79 for first year; $35 annually thereafter

Deposit: $500 minimum; can start initially with $100 and work up to $500

Account type: Savings at 4.0% interest

Grace period: 25 days

Review period: 1 year for additional credit; 2 years for unsecured card

Address: First National Bank
               PO Box 6000
               Brooking, SD 57006-6000

Phone: 1-800-847-2227

Key Federal Savings Bank

Card offered: Visa and MasterCard

Annual Percentage Rate: 18.9%

Fees: $35 annual fee

Deposit: $250 minimum

Account type: Savings at 4-4.5% interest

Grace period: 25-31 days

Review period: 24 months

Phone: 1-800-539-5398 (no need to write in:
they will send information to you if you request it by phone)

Marine Midland Bank

Card offered: MasterCard

Annual Percentage Rate: 19.8%

Fees: $35

Deposit: $300 minimum

Account type: Savings with interest at regular savings rate

Review period: one year

Address: Marine Midland Bank (or your local branch)
               PO Box 4705
               Buffalo, NY 14240
               Attn: Credit Dept.

Phone: 1-800-962-7463

Orchard Bank (will accept individuals in Chapter 13 — see below)

Card offered: Visa and MasterCard

Annual Percentage Rate: 18.9% interest rate for $35 annual fee card; 13.9% or prime plus 7% for the $45 annual fee card

Deposit: $400 for low fee Visa and MasterCard

Account type: Savings at 4% interest

Review period: After 18 months, accounts are automatically reviewed for an unsecured line

Address: Orchard Bank
           PO Box 19268
           Portland, OR 97280

Phone: 1-800-688-6830 or 503-245-9280

If an individual has filed Chapter 13, the plan must be discharged before applying for a secured card. However, Orchard Bank may accept applications if the individual is at least six months into the plan. The bank will request payment history regarding the Chapter 13 payments.

Orchard Bank has also introduced an unsecured Visa card. Interest on the card is 18.9%, with a $90 annual fee the first year and a $45 fee each year thereafter. The initial line of credit is $300. After making payments for six months, individuals are eligible for a $100 increase, then $200 increases every six months thereafter.

To qualify for the card, the applicant must have a permanent address, no recent delinquent payments and an income of $1,000/month or more. A Chapter 7 bankruptcy must be discharged and for Chapter 13, you must be 6 months into the plan.

Service One Corporation

Card offered: Visa and MasterCard

Annual Percentage Rate:
    21% interest charge on merchandise purchases
    24% interest charge for cash advances

Fees:
    $69 processing
    $39 annual

Deposit: $380 minimum

Account type: Savings at 4.5% interest

Address: Service One Corp.
                3401 N. Louise Ave.
                Sioux Falls, SD 57107
                Attn: Marketing Dept.

Phone: 605-338-5530

For a list of banks (more than 100 now offer secured credit cards) send $5 to:

Bankcard Holders of America
560 Herndon Parkway
Suite 120
Herndon, Virginia 22070

RAM Research also publishes a report on credit cards for $5 that includes a listing of secured cards.

CardTrak
Box 1700
Frederick, MD 21702

Please specify that you are requesting the "Secured credit card list."

Index

I

inheritance 45
insurance 37, 56

J

job status 94, 122-124
joint filing 7, 107
judge, bankruptcy 31, 67
judgment 6, 43, 95, 108

L

lien 69, 108
liquidation 108, 110, 114

M

medical bills 18, 38
meeting of creditors 8, 9-10, 28-30, 108
mortgage lenders 100, 119-121
mortgage payments 64-68
motor vehicles 10, 29, 69-70, 122-124

P

paralegal 104
pensions 21, 56
petition 7-9, 15-16, 18, 27-28, 34
profit-sharing plans 47
property, personal 55, 69
public assistance 53

R

reaffirmation 17, 70
real estate 10, 29, 31, 37, 54, 64-68, 113
rent 46, 94
retirement plans 47

S

secured credit cards 92-93, 125-128
secured debt 40, 108
self-employment 6, 40, 58
Social Security 44, 56
student loans 12, 80-86

T

taxes 12, 49, 54, 87-90
341 Meeting 8-10, 28-30, 34, 108
trustee 8-10, 21, 27-32, 59-60, 62, 109

U

unemployment 32, 40
unsecured debt 40, 109
utilities 94, 116-118

W

Workers' Compensation 56